LibreOffice Math 4.4

A catalogue record for this book is available from the Hong Kong Public Libraries.

Published by Samurai Media Limited.

Email: info@samuraimedia.org

ISBN 978-988-14435-6-4

Contents

Math Guide

Preface

Who is this book for?

LibreOffice Math is a formula (equation) editor that is an integral part of LibreOffice. Anyone who wants to learn how to insert formulas and equations using Math will find this guide valuable.

If you have never used LibreOffice Math before, or you want an introduction to all of the LibreOffice components, you might like to read the LibreOffice *Getting Started Guide* first.

Where to get more help

This guide, other LibreOffice user guides, the built-in Help system, and user support systems assume that you are familiar with your computer and basic functions such as starting a program, opening and saving files.

Help system

LibreOffice comes with an extensive Help system. This is your first line of support for using LibreOffice.

To display the full Help system, press *F1* or go to **Help > LibreOffice Help** on the main menu bar. In addition, you can choose whether to activate *Tips, Extended tips*, and the *Help Agent* by going to **Tools > Options > LibreOffice > General** on the main menu bar.

If *Tips* are enabled, hover the mouse pointer over any of the icons and a small balloon (tooltip) will pop up giving a brief explanation of the function for that icon. For a more detailed explanation, select **Help > What's This?** on the main menu bar and hover the pointer over the icon.

Free online support

The LibreOffice community not only develops software, but provides free, volunteer-based support. See Table 1 and this web page: http://www.libreoffice.org/get-help/

Table 1: Free support for LibreOffice users

Ask LibreOffice	Questions and answers from the LibreOffice community http://ask.libreoffice.org/en/questions/
Documentation	User guides, how-tos, and other documentation. http://www.libreoffice.org/get-help/documentation/ https://wiki.documentfoundation.org/Documentation/Publications
Mailing lists	Free community support is provided by a network of experienced users http://www.libreoffice.org/get-help/mailing-lists/
FAQs	Answers to frequently asked questions http://wiki.documentfoundation.org/Faq
International support	The LibreOffice website in your language. http://global.libreoffice.org/international-sites/ International mailing lists http://wiki.documentfoundation.org/Local_Mailing_Lists
Accessibility options	Information about available accessibility options. http://www.libreoffice.org/get-help/accessibility/

You can get comprehensive online support from the community through mailing lists and the Ask LibreOffice website, http://ask.libreoffice.org/en/questions/. Other websites run by users also offer free tips and tutorials. This forum provides community support for LibreOffice: http://en.libreofficeforum.org/. This site provides support for LibreOffice, among other programs: http://forum.openoffice.org/en/forum/

Paid support and training

Alternatively, you can pay for support services. Service contracts can be purchased from a vendor or consulting firm specializing in LibreOffice.

What you see may be different

LibreOffice runs on Windows, Linux, and Mac OS X operating systems, each of which has several versions and can be customized by users (fonts, colors, themes, window managers).

Illustrations

The illustrations in this guide were taken from a variety of computers and operating systems. Therefore, some illustrations will not look exactly like what you see on your computer display.

Also, some of the dialogs may be different because of the settings selected in LibreOffice. You can either use dialogs from your computer system or dialogs provided by LibreOffice. To change to using LibreOffice dialogs if settings have been altered:

1) Access the general options for LibreOffice as follows:
   - On Linux and Windows operating systems, go to **Tools > Options > LibreOffice > General** on the main menu bar to open the dialog for general options.
   - On a Mac operating system, go to **LibreOffice > Preferences > General** on the main menu bar to open the dialog for general options.
2) Select *Use LibreOffice dialogs* in **Open/Save dialogs** to display and use the LibreOffice dialogs for opening and saving files.
3) For Linux operating systems only, select *Use LibreOffice dialogs* in **Print Dialogs** to display and use the LibreOffice dialogs for printing your documents.
4) Click **OK** to save your settings and close the dialog.

> **Note**
>
> If you are using a Linux operating system as a virtual machine on a computer running a Windows or Mac operating system, then the LibreOffice option of using **Print Dialogs** is not available.

Icons

The icons used to illustrate some of the many tools available in LibreOffice may differ from the ones used in this guide. The icons in this guide have been taken from a LibreOffice installation that has been set to display the Galaxy set of icons. If you wish, you can change your LibreOffice software package to display Galaxy icons as follows:

1) Access the view options for LibreOffice as follows:
   - On Linux and Windows operating systems, go to **Tools > Options > LibreOffice > View** on the main menu bar to open the dialog for view options.
   - On a Mac operating system, go to **LibreOffice > Preferences > View** on the main menu bar to open the dialog for view options.
2) In **User interface**, select *Galaxy* from the options available in the *Icon size and style* drop-down list.
3) Click **OK** to save your settings and close the dialog.

NOTE

Some Linux operating systems, for example Ubuntu, include LibreOffice as part of the installation and may not include the Galaxy icon set. You should be able to download the Galaxy icon set from the software repository for your Linux operating system.

What are all these things called?

The terms used in LibreOffice for most parts of the user interface (the parts of the program you see and use, in contrast to the behind-the-scenes code that actually makes it work) are the same as for most other programs.

A *dialog* is a special type of window. Its purpose is to inform you of something, or request input from you, or both. It provides controls for you to use to specify how to carry out an action. The technical names for common controls are shown in Figure 1. In most cases we do not use the technical terms in this book, but it is useful to know them because the Help and other sources of information often use them.

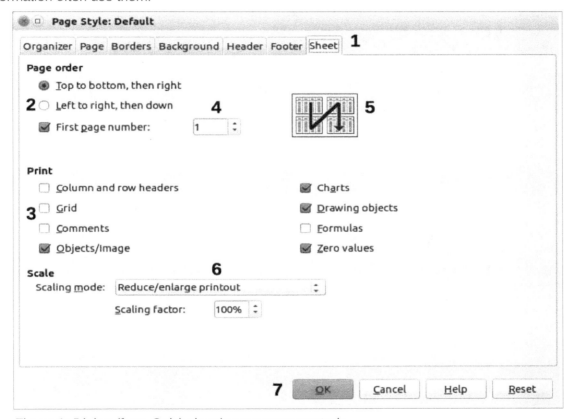

Figure 1: Dialog (from Calc) showing common controls

1) Tabbed page (not strictly speaking a control).
2) Radio buttons (only one can be selected at a time).
3) Checkbox (more than one can be selected at a time).
4) Spin box (click the up and down arrows to change the number shown in the text box next to it, or type in the text box).
5) Thumbnail or preview.
6) Drop-down list from which to select an item.
7) Push buttons.

In most cases, you can interact only with the dialog (not the document itself) as long as the dialog remains open. When you close the dialog after use (usually, clicking **OK** or another button saves your changes and closes the dialog), then you can again work with your document.

Some dialogs can be left open as you work, so you can switch back and forth between the dialog and your document. An example of this type is the Find & Replace dialog.

Using LibreOffice on a Mac

Some keystrokes and menu items are different on a Mac from those used in Windows and Linux. The table below gives some common substitutions for the instructions in this chapter. For a more detailed list, see the application Help.

Windows or Linux	Mac equivalent	Effect
Tools > Options menu selection	**LibreOffice > Preferences**	Access setup options
Right-click	*Control+click* or *right-click* depending on computer setup	Opens a context menu
Ctrl (Control)	⌘ *(Command)*	Used with other keys
F5	*Shift+⌘+F5*	Open the Navigator
F11	*⌘+T*	Open the Styles and Formatting window

Who wrote this book?

This book was written by volunteers from the LibreOffice community, as listed on the Copyright page. Profits from sales of the printed edition will be used to benefit the community.

Frequently asked questions

How is LibreOffice licensed?
LibreOffice is distributed under the Open Source Initiative (OSI) approved Mozilla Public License (MPL). The MPL license is available from http://www.mozilla.org/MPL/2.0/.

May I distribute LibreOffice to anyone?
Yes.

How many computers may I install it on?
As many as you like.

May I sell it?
Yes.

May I use LibreOffice in my business?
Yes.

Is LibreOffice available in my language?
LibreOffice has been translated (localized) into over 40 languages, so your language probably is supported. Additionally, there are over 70 *spelling*, *hyphenation*, and *thesaurus* dictionaries available for languages, and dialects that do not have a localized program interface. The dictionaries are available from the LibreOffice website at: www.libreoffice.org.

How can you make it for free?
LibreOffice is developed and maintained by volunteers and has the backing of several organizations.

How can I contribute to LibreOffice?
>   You can help with the development and user support of LibreOffice in many ways, and you do not need to be a programmer. To start, check out this webpage:
>   http://www.documentfoundation.org/contribution/

May I distribute the PDF of this book, or print and sell copies?
>   Yes, as long as you meet the requirements of one of the licenses in the copyright statement at the beginning of this book. You do not have to request special permission. In addition, we request that you share with the project some of the profits you make from sales of books, in consideration of all the work we have put into producing them.

What is new in LibreOffice 4.4?

The LibreOffice 4.4 Release Notes (changes from version 4.3) are here:
https://wiki.documentfoundation.org/ReleaseNotes/4.4.

You may also want to read the LibreOffice 4.3 Release Notes (changes from version 4.2):
https://wiki.documentfoundation.org/ReleaseNotes/4.3.

Math Guide

Chapter 1
Creating & Editing Formulas

Introduction

Math is a formula editor module included with LibreOffice that allows you to create or edit formulas (equations) in a symbolic form, within LibreOffice documents or as stand-alone objects; example formulas are shown below. However, if you want to evaluate numeric values using formulas, then refer to the *Calc Guide* for more information as Math does not carry out any actual calculation.

$$\frac{df(x)}{dx} = \ln(x) + \tan^{-1}(x^2) \quad \text{or} \quad NH_3 + H_2O \rightleftharpoons NH_4^+ + OH^-$$

The Formula Editor in Math uses a markup language to represent formulas. This markup language is designed to be easily read wherever possible, for example, a over b produces the fraction $\frac{a}{b}$ when used in a formula.

Getting started

Using the Formula Editor, you can create a formula as a separate document or file for a formula library, or insert formulas directly into a document using LibreOffice Writer, Calc, Impress or Draw.

Formulas as separate documents or files

To create a formula as a separate document or file, use one of the following methods to open an empty formula document in LibreOffice Math (Figure 2).

- On the main menu bar, go to **File > New > Formula**.

- On the Standard toolbar, click the triangle to the right of the **New** icon and select **Formula** from the context menu.

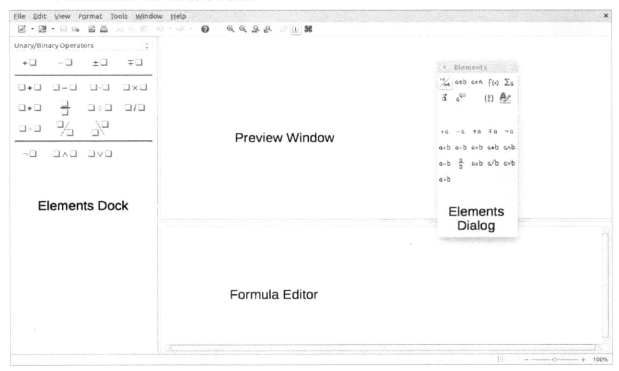

Figure 2: An empty formula document in Math

- From the Start Center, click **Math Formula**.
- From within LibreOffice Math, use the keyboard shortcut *Ctrl+N*.

As you enter the markup language in the Formula Editor, the formula will appear in the Preview window during and after input of the markup language. The Elements Dock to the left of the Preview window and/or the Elements dialog as a floating dialog may also appear, if these have been selected in **View** on the main menu bar. For more information on creating formulas, see "Creating formulas" on Page 19.

Formulas in LibreOffice documents

To insert a formula into a LibreOffice document, open the document in Writer, Calc, Draw, or Impress. The LibreOffice module you are using affects how you position the cursor to insert the formula.

- In Writer, click in the paragraph where you want to insert the formula.
- In Calc, click in the spreadsheet cell where you want to insert the formula.
- In Draw and Impress, the formula is inserted into the center of the drawing or slide.

Then, go to **Insert > Object > Formula** on the main menu bar to open the Formula Editor. Alternatively, go to **Insert > Object > OLE Object** on the main menu bar to open the Insert OLE Object dialog, select **Create new** option and *Formula* from the sub-menu, then click **OK** to open the Formula Editor. The Elements Dock to the left of the Preview window and/or the Elements dialog as a floating dialog may also appear, if these have been selected in **View** on the main menu bar. For more information on creating formulas, see "Creating formulas" on Page 19.

Figure 3 shows an example Writer document with the formula box selected ready for a formula to be entered.

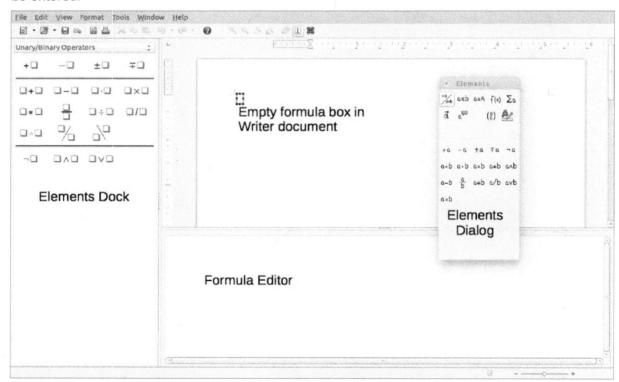

Figure 3: Empty formula in a Writer document

When you have completed entering the markup language for your formula, close the Formula Editor by pressing the *Esc* key or by clicking an area outside the formula in your document. Double-clicking on the formula object in your document will open the Formula Editor again so that you can edit the formula.

Formulas are inserted as OLE objects into documents. You can, as with any OLE object, change how the object is placed within your document. For more information on OLE objects, see *Chapter 2 Formulas in Writer*, *Chapter 3 Formulas in Calc, Draw & Impress* and the user guides for Writer, Calc, Draw, and Impress.

If you frequently insert formulas into documents, it is recommended to add the Formula button to the Standard toolbar or create a keyboard shortcut. See *Chapter 4 Customization* for more information.

Creating formulas

You can insert a formula using one of the following methods:

- Select a category, then a symbol using the Elements dialog.
- Select a category from the drop-down list, then a symbol using the Elements Dock.
- Right-click in the Formula Editor and select a category, then a symbol from the context menu.
- Enter markup language directly in the Formula Editor.

NOTE

Using the Elements dialog, Elements Dock, or the context menus to insert a formula provides a convenient way to learn the markup language used by LibreOffice Math.

Elements dialog

1) Go to **View > Elements** on the main menu bar to open the Elements dialog (Figure 4).
2) Select the category you want to use in your formula from the upper part of the Elements dialog.
3) Select the symbol you want to use in your formula from the bottom part of the Elements dialog. The symbols that are available change according to the selected category.

Figure 4: Elements dialog

Tip

When using the Elements dialog or the Elements Dock, it is recommended to have *Tips* selected in the LibreOffice Options. This will help you identify the categories and symbols you want to use in your formula. Go to **Tools > Options** on the main menu bar, then select **LibreOffice > General** in the Options dialog and select **Tips** in the *Help* section.

Elements Dock

The Elements Dock has the same categories as the Elements dialog and either can easily be used when entering your formula data. However, the Elements Dock also provides an Example category which gives you example formulas to use as a starting point for your formula or equation.

1) Go to **View** on the main menu bar and select **Elements Dock** to open the Elements Dock (Figure 5).

2) Select the category you want to use in your formula from the drop-down list at the top of the Elements Dock.

3) Select the symbol you want to use in your formula from the Elements Dock. The symbols that are available change according to the selected category.

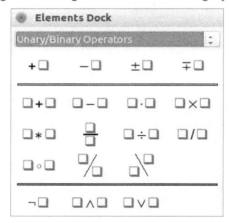

Figure 5: Elements Dock

NOTE

The Elements Dock can either be a floating dialog, as shown in Figure 5, or positioned to the left of the Formula Editor, as shown in Figure 2 and Figure 3.

Context menu

The Formula Editor also provides a context menu to access categories and symbols when creating your formula. Right-click in the Formula Editor to open the context menu. Select a category and then select the markup example that you want to use from the sub-context menu, an example is shown in Figure 6.

NOTE

The Elements dialog, Elements Dock, or context menu only contain the most common commands that are used in formulas. For some seldom-used commands, you must always enter the command using the markup language. For a complete list of commands, see *Appendix A Commands Reference*.

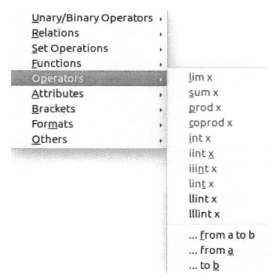

Figure 6: Context menu in Formula Editor

Markup language

Markup language is entered directly into the Formula Editor. For example, typing the markup language 5 `times` 4 into the Formula Editor creates the simple formula 5×4. If you are experienced in using markup language, it can be the quickest way to enter a formula. Table 2 shows some examples of using markup language to enter commands. For a full list of commands that can be used in the Formula Editor, see *Appendix A Commands Reference*.

Table 2: Example commands using markup language

Display	Command	Display	Command
$a = b$	`a = b`	$\sqrt{a}$	`sqrt {a}`
a^2	`a^2`	a_n	`a_n`
$\int f(x)\,dx$	`int f(x) dx`	$\sum a_n$	`sum a_n`
$a \leq b$	`a <= b`	∞	`infinity`
$a \times b$	`a times b`	$x \cdot y$	`x cdot y`

Greek characters

Using markup language

Greek characters are commonly used in formulas, but Greek characters cannot be entered into a formula using the Elements dialog, Elements Dock, or the context menu. Use the English names of Greek characters in markup language when entering Greek characters into a formula. See *Appendix A commands Reference* for a list of Greek characters that can be entered using markup language.

- For a lowercase Greek character, type a percentage % sign, then type the character name in lowercase using the English name. For example, typing %lambda creates the Greek character λ.

- For an UPPERCASE Greek character, type a percentage % sign, then type the character name in UPPERCASE using the English name. For example, typing %LAMBDA creates the Greek character Λ.

- For an *italic* Greek character, type a percentage % sign followed by the i character, then the English name of the Greek character in lower or UPPER case. For example, typing %iTHETA creates the *italic* Greek character Θ.

Symbols dialog

Greek characters can also be entered into a formula using the Symbols dialog.

1) Make sure your cursor is in the correct position in the Formula Editor.

2) Go to **Tools > Catalog** on the main menu bar or click on the **Catalog** icon 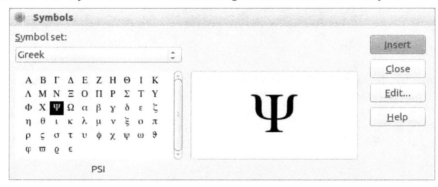 in the Tools toolbar to open the Symbols dialog (Figure 7)

3) Select *Greek* from the **Symbol set** drop-down list. For *italic* characters, select *iGreek* from the drop-down list.

4) Select the Greek character from the symbol list, then click **Insert**. When selected, the name of a Greek character is shown below the symbol list.

5) Click **Close** when you have finished entering Greek characters into your formula.

Figure 7: Symbols dialog

Formula examples

Example 1

The simple formula 5×4 can be created using LibreOffice Math as follows:

1) Make sure your cursor is flashing in the Formula Editor, then select the category **Unary/Binary Operators** and symbol **Multiplication** using one of the following methods:

   - In the Elements dialog, select the **Unary/Binary Operators** icon and then select the **Multiplication** icon $a \times b$.

   - In the Elements Dock, select **Unary/Binary Operators** from the drop-down list and then select the **Multiplication** icon $\square \times \square$.

   - Right-click in the Formula Editor and select **Unary/Binary Operators > a times b** from the context menu.

   - Using markup language, enter 5 `times` 4 in the Formula Editor.

   - The first three methods place the formula text <?> `times` <?> in the Formula Editor and the symbol $\square \times \square$ appears in the document.

   - Using markup language in the Formula Editor places the formula 5×4 directly into your document and there is no need to carry out the following steps.

2) Select the first placeholder <?> before the word `times` in the Formula Editor and replace it with the character 5. The formula in your document updates automatically.

3) Select the second placeholder <?> after the word `times` in the Formula Editor and replace it with the character 4. The formula in your document updates automatically.

Tip

To move forward from one placeholder to the next placeholder in a formula, press the *F4* key. To move backward from one placeholder to the previous placeholder in a formula, use the key combination *Shift+F4*.

NOTE

If necessary, you can prevent a formula in a document from updating automatically. Go to **View** on the main menu bar and deselect **AutoUpdate display**. To then manually update a formula, press *F9* key or select **View > Update** on the main menu bar.

Example 2

You want to enter the formula $\pi \simeq 3.14159$ where the value of pi is rounded to 5 decimal places. You know the name of the Greek character (pi), but do not know the markup associated with the `Is Similar Or Equal` symbol $\simeq$.

1) Make sure your cursor is flashing in the Formula Editor.

2) Enter %pi in the Formula Editor to enter the Greek character for pi (π).

3) Select the category **Relations** and symbol **Is Similar Or Equal** using one of the following methods:

   – In the Elements dialog, select the **Relations** icon $a \lessgtr b$ and then select the **Is Similar Or Equal** icon $a \approx b$.

   – In the Elements Dock, select **Relations** from the drop-down list and then select the **Is Similar Or Equal** icon $\square \approx \square$.

   – Right-click in the Formula Editor and select **Relations > a simeq b** from the context menu.

4) Delete the first placeholder <?> before the word `simeq` in the Formula Editor.

5) Select the second placeholder <?> after the word `simeq` in the Formula Editor and replace it with the characters 3.14159. The formula $\pi \simeq 3.14159$ now appears in your document.

Editing formulas

How you edit a formula and switch into formula editing mode depends on whether the formula is in Math or another LibreOffice module.

1) In Math, double-click on a formula element in the formula that appears in the Preview window to select the formula element in the Formula Editor, or directly select a formula element in the Formula Editor.

2) In Writer, Calc, Impress, or Draw, double-click on the formula, or right-click on the formula and select **Edit** form the context menu, to open the Formula Editor and enter editing mode. The cursor is positioned at the start of the formula in the Formula Editor.

NOTE

If you cannot select a formula element using your cursor, click on the **Formula Cursor** icon ⊥ in the Tools toolbar to activate the formula cursor.

3) Select the formula element you want to change use one of the following methods:
   - Click on the formula element in the preview window positioning the cursor at the beginning of the formula element in the Formula Editor, then select the formula element in the Formula Editor.
   - Double-click on the formula element in the preview window to select the formula element in the Formula Editor.
   - Position the cursor in the Formula Editor at the formula element you want to edit, then select that formula element.
   - Double-click directly on the formula element in the Formula Editor to select it.
4) Make your changes to the formula element you have selected.
5) Go to **View > Update** on the main menu bar, or press the *F9* key, or click on the **Update** icon 🗘 in the Tools toolbar to update the formula in the preview window or your document.
6) In Math, save your changes to the formula after editing.
7) In Writer, Calc, Impress or Draw, click anywhere in your document away from the formula to leave editing mode, then save your document to save your changes to the formula.

Formula layout

This section provides some advice on how to layout complex formulas in Math or in your LibreOffice document.

Using braces

LibreOffice Math knows nothing about order of operation within a formula. You must use braces (curly brackets) to state the order of operations that occur within a formula. The following examples show how braces can be used in a formula.

Example 1

2 over x + 1 gives the result $\frac{2}{x}+1$

Math has recognized that the 2 before and the x after the over as belonging to the fraction, and has represented them accordingly. If you want x+1 rather than x to be the denominator, you must bracket them together using braces so that both will be placed there.

Inserting braces into 2 over {x + 1} gives the result $\frac{2}{x+1}$ where x+1 is now the denominator.

Example 2

- 1 over 2 gives the result $\frac{-1}{2}$

Math has recognized the minus sign as a prefix for the 1 and has therefore placed it in the numerator of the fraction. If you wish to show that the whole fraction is negative, with the minus sign in front of the fraction, you must put the fraction in braces to signify to Math that the characters belong together.

Adding braces into the markup language {1 over 2} gives the result $-\frac{1}{2}$ and the whole fraction is now negative.

Example 3

   When braces are used in markup language, they are used to define the layout of the formula and are not displayed or printed. If you want to use braces within your formula, you use the commands `lbrace` and `rbrace` within the markup language.

   `x over {-x + 1}` gives the result $\dfrac{x}{-x+1}$

   Replace the braces using the commands `lbrace` and `rbrace` in the markup language.

   Write `x over lbrace -x + 1 rbrace` and the result is $\dfrac{x}{\{-x+1\}}$

Brackets (parentheses) and matrices

If you want to use a matrix in a formula, you have to use a matrix command. For example, `matrix { a # b ## c # d }` gives the resulting matrix $\begin{matrix} a & b \\ c & d \end{matrix}$ in your formula, where rows are separated by two hashes (##) and entries within each row are separated by one hash (#).

Normally, when you use brackets within a matrix, the brackets do not scale as the matrix increases in size. For example, `( matrix { a # b ## c # d } )` gives the result $\left(\begin{matrix} a & b \\ c & d \end{matrix}\right.$

To overcome this problem of brackets with a matrix, LibreOffice Math provides scalable brackets that grow in size to match the size a matrix. The commands `left(` and `right)` have to be used to create scalable brackets within a matrix. For example, `left( matrix { a # b ## c # d } right)` gives the result $\left(\begin{matrix} a & b \\ c & d \end{matrix}\right)$ where the matrix is now bracketed by scalable brackets.

Scalable brackets can also be used with any element of a formula, such as fraction, square root, and so on.

> **Tip**
>
> Use the commands `left[` and `right]` to obtain square brackets. A list of all brackets available within Math can be found in *Appendix A Commands Reference*.

> **Tip**
>
> If you want all brackets to be scalable, go to **Format > Spacing** to open the Spacing dialog. Click on **Category**, select *Brackets* from the drop-down list and then select the option **Scale all brackets**.

Unpaired brackets

When using brackets in a formula, Math expects that for every opening bracket there will be a closing one. If you forget to add a closing bracket, Math places an inverted question mark next to where the closing bracket should have been placed. This inverted question mark disappears when all the brackets are paired. However, an unpaired bracket is sometimes necessary and you have the following options.

Non-scalable brackets

A backslash \ is placed before a nonscalable bracket to indicate that the following character should not be regarded as a bracket, but as a literal character.

For example, the unpaired brackets in the formula [a; b [are deliberate, but gives the result $a;b¿$. To remove the inverted question marks and create unpaired brackets, backslashes are added. The formula now becomes \ [a; b \ [and the result $[a;b[$ shows unpaired brackets without the inverted question marks.

Scalable brackets

To create unpaired scalable brackets or braces in a formula, the markup commands left, right, and none are used.

Example

You want to create the formula $|x| = \begin{cases} x \text{ for } x \geq 0 \\ -x \text{ for } x < 0 \end{cases}$ and in the Formula Editor you enter abs = x lbrace stack {x "for" x >= 0 # -x "for" x < 0. However, this gives the incorrect result $\begin{matrix} ¿ \\ x \text{ for } x \geq 0 \\ -x \text{ for } x < 0 \end{matrix}$. To remove the inverted question marks and create the correct formula, you have to use the markup commands left, right, and none. Change your entry in the Formula Editor to abs x = left lbrace stack {x "for" x >= 0 # -x "for" x < 0} right none and this creates the correct formula.

Recognizing functions

In the basic installation of Math, Math outputs functions in normal characters and variables in *italic* characters. However, if Math fails to recognize a function, you can tell Math that you have just entered a function. Enter the markup command func before a function forces Math to recognize the following text as a function and uses normal characters.

For a full list of functions within Math, see *Appendix A Commands Reference*.

Some Math functions have to be followed by a number or a variable. If these are missing, Math places an inverted question mark where the missing number or variable should be. To remove the inverted question mark and correct the formula, you have to enter a number, a variable or a pair of empty brackets as a placeholder.

> **Tip**
>
> You can navigate through errors in a formula using the key *F3* or the key combination *Shift+F3*.

Formulas over multiple lines

Suppose you want to create a formula that requires more than one line, for example $\begin{matrix} x=3 \\ y=1 \end{matrix}$. Your first reaction would normally be to press the *Enter* key. However, if you press the *Enter* key, the markup language in the Formula Editor goes to a new line, but the resulting formula does not have two lines. You must type the macro command newline each time you want to create and display a new line in a formula.

Example
```
x = 3
y = 1
```
gives the incorrect result $x=3\ y=1$

x = 3 newline y = 1 gives the correct result $\begin{matrix} x=3 \\ y=1 \end{matrix}$

It is not possible in Math to create multiple line formulas when a line ends with an equals sign and you want to continue the calculation on a new line without completing the term on the right side of the equals sign. If you require a multiple line formula to have an equals sign at the end of a line without a term after the equals sign, then use either empty quotes "" or empty braces {} or the space characters grave ` or tilde ~.

By default, the alignment of a multiple line formula is center aligned. For more information on alignment using the equals sign, see *Chapter 4 Customization*.

Spacing between the element in a formula is not set by using space characters in the markup language. If you want to add spaces into your formula, use one of the following options:

- Grave ` to add a small space.
- Tilde ~ for a large space.
- Add space characters between quotes " ". These spaces will be considered as text.

Any spaces at the end of a line in the markup language are ignored by default. For more information, see *Chapter 4 Customization*.

Adding limits to sum/integral commands

The sum and integral commands can take the parameters `from` and `to` if you want to set the lower and upper limits respectively. The parameters `from` and `to` can be used singly or together as shown by the following examples. For more information on the sum and integral commands, see *Appendix A Commands Reference*.

Examples

`sum from k = 1 to n a_k` gives the result $\sum_{k=1}^{n} a_k$

`int from 0 to x f(t) dt` gives the result $\int_{0}^{x} f(t)\,dt$

`int_0^x f(t) dt` gives the result $\int_{0}^{x} f(t)\,dt$

`int from Re f` gives the result $\int_{\Re} f$

`sum to infinity 2^{-n}` gives the result $\sum^{\infty} 2^{-n}$

Writing derivatives

When writing derivatives, you have to tell Math that it is a fraction by using the `over` command. The `over` command is combined with the character d for a total derivative or the `partial` command for a partial derivative to achieve the effect of a derivative. Braces {} are used each side of the element to surround the element and make the derivative as shown by the following examples.

Examples

`{df} over {dx}` gives the result $\dfrac{df}{dx}$

`{partial f} over {partial y}` gives the result $\dfrac{\partial f}{\partial y}$

`{partial^2 f} over {partial t^2}` gives the result $\dfrac{\partial^2 f}{\partial t^2}$

Note

To write function names with primes, as is normal in school notation, you must first add the symbols to the catalog. See *Chapter 4 Customization* for more information.

Markup language characters as normal characters

Characters that are used as controls in markup language cannot be entered directly as normal characters. These characters are: %, {, }, &, |, _, ^ and ". For example, you cannot write 2% = 0.02 in markup language and expect the same characters to appear in your formula. To overcome this limitation in markup language, use one of the following methods:

- Use double quotes either side of the character to mark that character as text, for example 2"%"= 0.02 will appear in your formula as $2\%=0.02$. However, this method cannot be used for the double-quote character itself, see "Text in formulas" below.

- Add the character to the Math Catalog, for example the double quote character.

- Use commands, for example lbrace and rbrace give you literal braces $\{\}$.

Note

The Special Characters dialog used by other LibreOffice modules is not available in Math. If you are going to regularly require special characters in Math, then it is recommended to add the characters to the Math Catalog, see *Chapter 4 Customization* for more information.

Text in formulas

To include text in a formula, you have to enclose any text in double-quotes, for example x " for " x >= 0 in markup language will create the formula $x \text{ for } x \geq 0$. All characters, except double quotes, can be used in text. However, if you require double quotes in your formula text, then you have to create your text with double quotes in LibreOffice Writer, then copy and paste the text into the Formula Editor as shown in Figure 8.

The font used for text in a formula will be the default font that has been set in the Fonts dialog. For more information on how to change fonts used for in formulas, see "Changing formula appearance" on page 29.

By default, text alignment is left-justified in formulas. For more information on how to change text alignment, see "Adjusting formula alignment" on page 34.

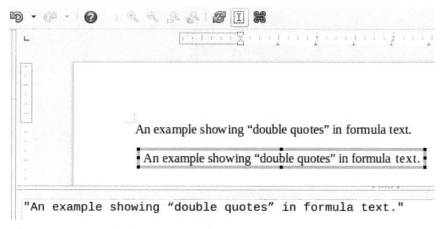

Figure 8: Example of double quotes in formula text

Formatting commands are not interpreted within text used in formulas. If you want to use formatting commands within formula text, then you must break up the text using double quotes in the Formula Editor.

Example

Enter the following in the Formula Editor:

```
"In " color blue bold "isosceles" "triangles, the base angles are equal"
```

creates the following text in a formula   In **isosceles** triangles, the base angles are equal

Aligning formulas using equals sign

LibreOffice Math does not have a command for aligning formulas on a particular character. However, you can use a matrix to align formulas on a character and this character is normally the equals sign (=).

Example

Creating the matrix:

```
matrix{ alignr x+y # {}={} # alignl 2 ## alignr x   # {}={} # alignl 2-y }
```

gives the following result where formulas are aligned on the equals sign $\begin{matrix} x+y & = & 2 \\ x & = & 2-y \end{matrix}$

Note

The empty braces each side of the equals sign are necessary because the equals sign is a binary operator and requires an expression on each side. You can use spaces, or ` or ~ characters each side of the equals sign, but braces are recommended as they are easier to see within the markup language.

You can reduce the spacing on each side of the equals sign if you change the inter-column spacing of the matrix. See "Adjusting formula spacing" on page 32 for information on how to adjust adjust formula spacing.

Changing formula appearance

Formula font size

Current formula font size

To change the font size used for a formula already inserted in Math or another LibreOffice module:

1) Click in the markup language in the Formula Editor.

2) Go to **Format > Font size** on the main menu bar to open the Font Sizes dialog (Figure 9).

3) Select a different font size using the *Base size* spinner or type a new font size in the *Base Size* box.

4) Click **OK** to save your changes and close the dialog. An example result when you change font size is shown below.

Example

Default font size 12pt: $\pi \simeq 3.14159$

After font size change to 18pt: $\pi \simeq 3.14159$

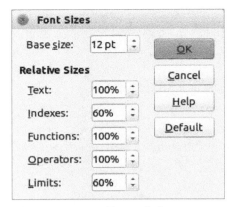

Figure 9: Font Sizes dialog

Default formula font size

To change the default font size used for all formulas in Math or another LibreOffice module:

1) Before inserting any formulas in your document, go to **Format > Font size** on the main menu bar to open the Font Sizes dialog (Figure 9).

2) Select a different font size using the Base size spinner or type a new font size in the *Base Size* box.

3) Click **Default** and confirm your changes to the base size font. Any formulas created from this point on will use the new base size font for formulas.

4) Click **OK** to save your changes and close the Font Sizes dialog.

> **Note**
>
> If you have already inserted formulas into your document and you change the default font size, only formulas inserted after the change in default font size will use the new default settings. You have to individually change the font size of formulas already inserted if you want these formulas to use the same font size as the default settings.

Font size options

The Font Sizes dialog (Figure 9) specifies the font sizes for your formula. Select a base size and all elements of the formula will be scaled in relation to this base.

- **Base size** – all elements of a formula are proportionally scaled to the base size. To change the base size, select or type in the desired point (pt) size. You can also use other units of measure or other metrics, which are then automatically converted to points.

- **Relative Sizes** – in this section, you can determine the relative sizes for each type of element with reference to the base size.

   - *Text* – select the size for text in a formula relative to the base size.

   - *Indexes* – select the relative size for the indexes in a formula in proportion to the base size.

   - *Functions* – select the relative size for names and other function elements in a formula in proportion to the base size.

   - *Operators* – select the relative size of the mathematical operators in a formula in proportion to the base size.

   - *Limits* – select the relative size for the limits in a formula in proportion to the base size.

- **Default** – clicking this button saves any changes as a default for all new formulas. A confirmation message appears before saving any changes.

Formula fonts

Current formula fonts

To change the fonts used for the current formula in Math or another LibreOffice module:

1) Click in the markup language in the Formula Editor.
2) Go to **Format > Fonts** on the main menu bar to open the Fonts dialog (Figure 10).
3) Select a new font for each the various options from the drop-down lists.
4) If the font you want to use does not appear in the drop-down list, click **Modify** and select the option from the context menu to open a fonts dialog. Select the font you want to use and click **OK** to add it to the drop-down list for that option.
5) Click **OK** to save your changes and close the Fonts dialog.

Figure 10: Fonts dialog

Default formula fonts

To change the default fonts used for all formulas in Math or another LibreOffice module:

1) Before inserting any formulas in your document, go to **Format > Fonts** on the main menu bar to open the Fonts dialog (Figure 10).
2) Select a new font for each the various options from the drop-down lists.
3) If the font you want to use does not appear in the drop-down list, click **Modify** and select the option from the context menu to open a fonts dialog. Select the font you want to use and click **OK** to add it to the drop-down list for that option.
4) Click **Default** and confirm your changes to the fonts. Any formulas created from this point on will use the new font for formulas.
5) Click **OK** to save your changes and close the Fonts dialog.

Note

If you have already inserted formulas into your document and you change the default fonts, only formulas inserted after the change in default fonts will use the new default settings. You have to individually change the font of formulas already inserted if you want these formulas to use the same font as the default settings.

Formula font options

Defines the fonts that can be applied to formula elements.

*   **Formula Fonts** – defines the fonts used for the variables, functions, numbers and inserted text that form the elements of a formula.

- *Variables* – selects the fonts for the variables in your formula. For example, in the formula x=SIN(y), x and y are variables and will reflect the assigned font.

- *Functions* – selects the fonts for names and properties of functions. For example, the functions in the formula x=SIN(y) are =SIN( ).

- *Numbers* – selects the fonts for the numbers in a formula.

- *Text* – defines the fonts for the text in a formula.

• **Custom Fonts** – in this section of the Fonts dialog (Figure 10), fonts are defined which format other text components in a formula. The three basic fonts Serif, Sans and Fixed are available. Other fonts can be added to each standard installed basic font using the **Modify** button. Every font installed on a computer system is available for use.

- *Serif* – specifies the font to be used for the font serif format. Serifs are the small "guides" that can be seen, for example, at the bottom of a capital A when the Times serif font is used. Using serifs is quite helpful since it guides the eye of a reader in a straight line and can speed up reading.

- *Sans* – specifies the font to be used for sans font formatting.

- *Fixed* – specifies the font to be used for fixed font formatting.

• **Modify** – click one of the options from the context menu to access the Fonts dialog, where the font and attributes can be defined for the respective formula and for custom fonts.

• ***Default*** – clicking this button saves any changes as a default for all new formulas. A confirmation message appears before saving any changes.

Note

When a new font is selected for a formula, the old font remains in the list alongside the new one and can be selected again.

Note

Variables should be written in *italics*, so make sure that the *Italic* option is selected. For the font you want to use. For all other elements, use the basic form of a font. The style can be easily altered in the formula itself by using the commands `italic` or `bold` to set these characteristics and `nitalic` or `nbold` to unset them.

Adjusting formula spacing

Use the Spacing dialog (Figure 11) to determine the spacing between formula elements. The spacing is specified as a percentage in relation to the defined base size for font sizes.

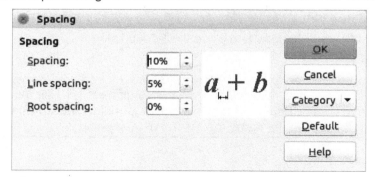

Figure 11: Spacing dialog

Current formula spacing

To change the spacing used for the current formula in Math or another LibreOffice module:

1) Click in the markup language in the Formula Editor.
2) Go to **Format > Spacing** on the main menu bar to open the Spacing dialog (Figure 11).
3) Click **Category** and select one of the options from the drop-down list. The options in the Spacing dialog change according to the category selected.
4) Enter new values for the spacing category and click **OK**.
5) Check the result in your formula. If not to your satisfaction, repeat the above steps.

Default formula spacing

To change the default spacing used for all formulas in Math or another LibreOffice module:

1) Before inserting any formulas in your document, go to **Format > Spacing** on the main menu bar to open the Spacing dialog (Figure 11).
2) Click **Category** and select one of the options from the drop-down list. The options in the Spacing dialog change according to the category selected.
3) Click **Default** and confirm your changes to the formula spacing. Any formulas created from this point on will use the new spacing for formulas.
4) Click **OK** to save your changes and close the Spacing dialog.

> **Note**
>
> If you have already inserted formulas into your document and you change the spacing, only formulas inserted after the change in spacing will use the new default settings. You have to individually change the spacing of formulas already inserted if you want these formulas to use the same spacing as the default settings.

Spacing options

Use Category in the Spacing dialog (Figure 11) to determine the formula element for which you would like to specify the spacing. The appearance of the dialog depends on the selected category. A preview window shows you which spacing is modified through the respective boxes.

*   **Category** – pressing this button allows you to select the category for which you would like to change the spacing.
*   **Spacing** – defines the spacing between variables and operators, between lines, and between root signs and radicals.
    *   *Line Spacing* – determines the spacing between lines.
    *   *Root Spacing* – determines the spacing between the root sign and radicals.
*   **Indexes** – defines the spacing for superscript and subscript indexes.
    *   *Superscript* – determines the spacing for superscript indexes.
    *   *Subscript* – determines the spacing for subscript indexes.
*   **Fractions** – defines the spacing between the fraction bar and the numerator or denominator.
    *   *Numerator* – determines the spacing between the fraction bar and the numerator.
    *   *Denominator* – determines the spacing between the fraction bar and the denominator.
*   **Fraction Bars** – defines the excess length and line weight of the fraction bar.
    *   *Excess length* – determines the excess length of the fraction line.
    *   *Weight* – determines the weight of the fraction line.

- **Limits** – defines the spacing between the sum symbol and the limit conditions.
  - *Upper limit* – determines the spacing between the sum symbol and the upper limit.
  - *Lower limit* – determines the spacing between the sum symbol and the lower limit.
- **Brackets** – defines the spacing between brackets and the content.
  - *Excess size (left/right)* – determines the vertical distance between the upper edge of the contents and the upper end of the brackets.
  - *Spacing* – determines the horizontal distance between the contents and the upper end of the brackets.
  - *Scale all brackets* – scales all types of brackets. If you then enter (a over b) in the Formula Editor, the brackets will surround the whole height of the argument. You normally achieve this effect by entering left (a over b right).
  - *Excess size* – adjusts the percentage excess size. At 0% the brackets are set so that they surround the argument at the same height. The higher the entered value is, the larger the vertical gap between the contents of the brackets and the external border of the brackets. The field can only be used in combination with *Scale all brackets*.
- **Matrices** – defines the relative spacing for the elements in a matrix.
  - *Line spacing* – determines the spacing between matrix elements in a row.
  - *Column spacing* – determines the spacing between matrix elements in a column.
- **Symbols** – defines the spacing of symbols in relation to variables
  - *Primary height* – defines the height of the symbols in relation to the baseline.
  - *Minimum spacing* – determines the minimum distance between a symbol and variable.
- **Operators** – defines the spacing between operators and variables or numbers.
  - *Excess size* – determines the height from the variable to the operator upper edge.
  - *Spacing* – determines the horizontal distance between operators and variables.
- **Borders** – adds a border to a formula. This option is particularly useful if you want to integrate the formula into a text file in LibreOffice Writer. When making settings, make sure that you do not use 0 as a size as this creates viewing problems for text that surrounds the insertion point.
  - *Left* – the left border is positioned between the formula and background.
  - *Right* – the right border is positioned between the formula and background.
  - *Top* – the top border is positioned between the formula and background.
  - *Bottom* – the bottom border is positioned between the formula and background.
- **Preview Field** – displays a preview of the current selection.
- **Default** – saves any changes as default settings for all new formulas. A security response will appear before saving these changes.

Adjusting formula alignment

The alignment settings determine how formula elements located above one another are aligned horizontally relative to each other.

Note

It is not possible to align formulas on a particular character and formula alignment does not apply to text elements. Text elements are always aligned left.

Note

Independent of using formula alignment given below, it is possible to align formulas using the commands `alignl`, `alignc` and `alignr`. These commands also work for text elements.

Current formula alignment

To change the alignment used for the current formula in Math or another LibreOffice module:

1) Click in the markup language in the Formula Editor.

2) Go to **Format > Alignment** on the main menu bar to open the Alignment dialog (Figure 12).

3) Select either *Left*, *Centered*, or *Right* for horizontal alignment.

4) Click **OK** and check the result in your formula. If not to your satisfaction, repeat the above steps.

Figure 12: Alignment dialog

Default formula alignment

To change the default alignment used for all formulas in Math or another LibreOffice module:

1) Before inserting any formulas in your document, go to **Format > Alignment** on the main menu bar to open the Alignment dialog (Figure 12).

2) Select either *Left*, *Centered*, or *Right* for horizontal alignment.

3) Click **Default** and confirm your changes to the formula alignment. Any formulas created from this point on will use the new alignment for formulas.

4) Click **OK** and check the result in your formula. If not to your satisfaction, repeat the above steps.

Note

If you have already inserted formulas into your document and you change the formula alignment, only formulas inserted after the change in alignment will use the new default settings. You have to individually change the alignment of formulas already inserted if you want these formulas to use the same alignment as the default settings.

Changing formula color

Character color

Formula color for the characters used in a formula is changed by using the command `color` in the mark up language. This command only works on the formula element immediately after the color name. For example, entering the markup language `color red ABC 5 times 4` gives the result $ABC\,5\times4$.

To change the color of the whole formula, you have to enclose the whole formula within brackets. For example, entering the markup language `color red {ABC 5 times 4}` gives the result $ABC5 \times 4$.

For information on the colors available in Math, see *Appendix A Commands Reference*.

Background color

It is not possible to select a background color for formulas in LibreOffice Math. The background color for a formula is by default the same color as the document or frame that the formula has been inserted into. However, in LibreOffice documents, you can use object properties to change the background color for a formula. For more information on using a background color (area fill for objects) with a formula, please refer to the user guides for Writer, Calc, Draw and Impress.

Formula library

If you regularly insert the same formulas into your documents, you can create a formula library using formulas that you have created using the Formula Editor. Individual formulas can be saved as separate files using the ODF format for formulas with the file suffix of `.odf`, or in MathML format with the file suffix of `.mml`.

You can use either LibreOffice Math, Writer, Calc, Draw, or Impress to create formulas and build up your formula library.

Using Math

1) Create a folder on your computer to contain your formulas and give the folder a memorable name, for example Formula Library.

2) In LibreOffice, go to **File > New > Formula** on the main menu bar, or click on **Math Formula** in the opening splash screen to open LibreOffice Math and create your formula using the Formula Editor. See "Formulas as separate documents or files" on Page 17 for more information.

3) Go to File > Save As on the main main menu bar or use the keyboard shortcut *Ctrl+Shift+S* to open a Save As dialog.

4) Navigate to the folder you have created for your formula library.

5) Type in a memorable name for your formula in the **File name** text box.

6) Select from the drop-down list for **File type** either *ODF Formula (.odf)* or *MathML 1.01 (.mml)* as the file type for your formula.

7) Click **Save** to save your formula and close the Save As dialog.

Using Writer, Calc, Draw, or Impress

1) Create a folder on your computer to contain your formulas and give the folder a memorable name, for example Formula Library.

2) Open a document using Writer, Calc, Draw, or Impress.

3) Go to **Insert > Object > Formula** on the main menu bar to open the Formula Editor and create your formula. See "Formulas in LibreOffice documents" on page 18 for more information.

4) Right-click on your formula object and select **Save Copy as** from the context menu to open a Save As dialog.

5) Navigate to the folder you have created for your formula library.

6) Type in a memorable name for your formula in the **File name** text box.

7) Select from the drop-down list for **File type** either *ODF Formula (.odf)* or *MathML 1.01 (.mml)* as the file type for your formula.

8) Click **Save** to save your formula and close the Save As dialog.

Using your formula library

You cannot insert a formula from your library into a document by dragging and dropping using the mouse, nor by using Insert > File on the main menu bar. You must insert a formula from your library into your document as an OLE object.

1) Open your document in Writer, Calc, Draw, or Impress.

2) Go to **Insert > Object > OLE Object** on the main menu bar to open the Insert OLE Object dialog.

3) Select the option **Create from file**.

4) Click **Search** to open your file browser dialog.

5) Navigate to the folder you have created for your formula library.

6) Select the formula you want to insert and click **Open**, or double-click on the formula you want to insert.

7) Click **OK** to insert your formula as an OLE object in your document and close the OLE Object dialog.

Math Guide

Chapter 2
Formulas in Writer

Introduction

When a formula is inserted into a document, LibreOffice Writer inserts the formula into a frame and treats the formula as an OLE object. Double-clicking on an inserted formula will open the Formula Editor in LibreOffice Math allowing you to edit the formula. For more information on creating and editing formulas, please refer to *Chapter 1 Creating & Editing Formulas*.

This chapter explains what options you can change for each individual formula within your Writer document. Please refer to the chapters on styles in the *Writer Guide* for information on how to change the default settings for frame styles for OLE objects.

Automatic formula numbering

Automatic numbering of formulas for cross reference purposes can only be carried out in LibreOffice Writer.

Numbering

1) Start a new line in your document.

2) Type *fn* and then press the *F3* key. A two column table with no borders is inserted into your document with the left column containing a sample formula and the right column containing a reference number, as shown below.

$$ABC\,5\times4 \hspace{10em} (1)$$

3) Delete the sample formula and insert your formula as an object in the left column. See *Chapter 1 Creating & Editing Formulas* for more information on inserting formulas.

4) Alternatively, you can first insert your formula into the document, then carry Steps 1 and 2 above replacing the sample formula with your formula.

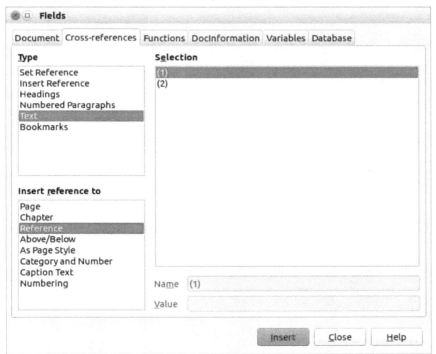

Figure 13: Fields dialog – Cross references page

Cross referencing

1) Click in your document where you want the cross reference to appear.
2) Go to **Insert > Cross-reference** on the menu bar to open the Fields dialog (Figure 13).
3) Click on the **Cross-references** tab, then select *Text* in the **Type** section.
4) In the **Selection** section, select the formula number you want to refer to.
5) In the **Insert reference to** section, select *Reference* and click **Insert**.
6) When you have finished creating cross references, click **Close** to close the Fields dialog.

Tip

To insert the cross reference number without parentheses, select *Numbering* instead of *Reference* in the **Insert** reference to section.

Note

If you want to use square parentheses instead of round ones, or if you want the cross reference number to be separated from the formula by tabs instead of using a table, then refer to the chapter on automatic text in the *Writer Guide*.

Anchoring formulas

A formula is treated as an object within Writer and its default anchoring is **As character** within a paragraph when it is inserted into a document. To change the anchoring of a formula object:

1) Right-click on the selected formula object and select **Anchor** from the context menu.
2) Select a new anchoring option from the context sub-menu. The anchoring positions available are **To page**, **To paragraph**, **To character** or **As character**.

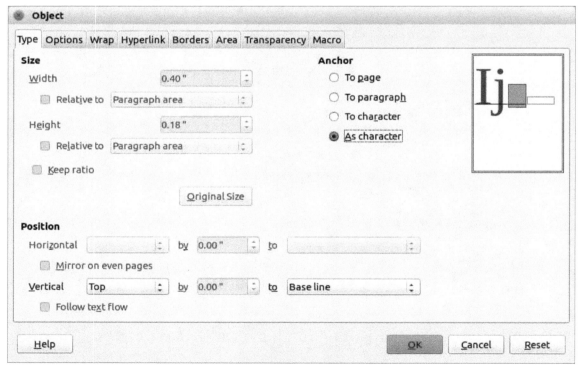

Figure 14: Object dialog – Type page with Anchor options

3) Alternatively, right-click on the selected formula object and select **Object** from the context menu, or go to **Format > Frame/Object** on the main menu bar to open the Object dialog (Figure 14).

4) Make sure the **Type** page is selected and select a new anchoring position from the *Anchor* section.

5) Click **OK** to save your changes and close the Object dialog.

Note

The anchoring options are not available in the Object dialog when you are making changes to the various options available for frame styles. For more information on how to modify frame styles, please refer to the chapters on styles in the *Writer Guide*.

Vertical alignment

The normal default setting for vertical alignment for formula objects is to use the text base line as a reference. This default setting can be changed by modifying the formula frame style, see the chapters on styles in the *Writer Guide* for more information.

To change the vertical alignment position of an individual formula object:

1) Right-click on the selected formula object and select **Object** from the context menu, or go to **Format > Frame/Object** to open the Object dialog (Figure 14).

2) Make sure the **Type** page is selected and select a new alignment position from the drop-down list in the *Position* section. The vertical alignment options available are **Top**, **Bottom**, **Center** or **From bottom**.

3) If necessary, type in the text box a plus or minus value for vertical alignment. This option is only available if **From bottom** vertical alignment has been selected.

4) Select the type of text alignment from the drop-down list in the *Position* section. The text alignment options available are **Base line**, **Character** and **Row**.

5) Click **OK** to save your changes and close the Object dialog.

Note

If the *Position* section in the Object dialog is greyed out and not available, then go to **Tools > Options > LibreOffice Writer > Formatting Aids** and uncheck the option *Math baseline alignment*. This setting is stored with the document and applies to all formulas within it. Any new documents created will also use this setting for *Math baseline alignment*.

Object spacing

A formula object, when inserted into a Writer document, has spacing each side of the formula object. The default value used for spacing is set within the frame style for formula objects and can be changed by modifying the formula frame style, see the chapters on styles in the *Writer Guide* for more information.

You can individually adjust the spacing for each formula object within your document as follows:

1) Create your formula in your Writer document.

2) Right-click on your selected formula object and select **Object** from the context menu, or go to **Format > Frame/Object** on the main menu bar to open the Object dialog.

3) Click on the **Wrap** tab to open the Wrap page in the Object dialog (Figure 15).

4) In the **Spacing** section, enter the spacing value for *Left*, *Right*, *Top* and *Bottom* spacing.

5) Click **OK** to save your changes and close the Object dialog.

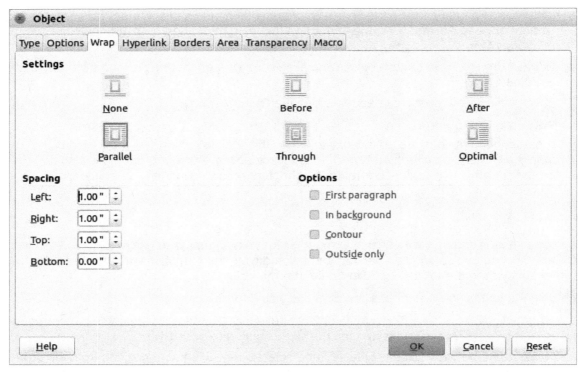

Figure 15: Object dialog – Wrap page

Text mode

In large formulas placed within a line of text, the formula elements can often be higher than the text height. Therefore, to make large formulas easier to read, it is recommended to always insert large formulas into a separate paragraph of their own so that it is separated from text.

However, if it is necessary to place a large formula within a line of text, double-click on the formula to open the Formula Editor and then go to **Format > Text Mode** on the main menu bar. The Formula Editor will try to shrink the formula to fit the text height. The numerators and denominators of fractions are shrunk, and the limits of integrals and sums are placed beside the integral/sum sign, as shown in the following example.

Example

A formula in a separate paragraph:

$$\sum_{i=2}^{5} i^2$$

and the same formula embedded into a line of text using text mode format: $\sum_{i=2}^{5} i^2$

Background and borders

The default setting for background (area fill) and borders for formula objects is set by the formula frame style. To change this default setting for formula frame style, refer to the chapters on styles in the *Writer Guide*. However, for individual formulas in your document, you can change the background and borders.

Note

The size of the frame that a formula is placed in when inserted into a document cannot be changed. The frame size for a formula object depends on the setting of the formula font size, see *Chapter 1 Creating & Editing Formulas* for more information.

Backgrounds

1) In your document, select the formula where you want to change the background.

2) Right-click on the formula and select **Object** from the context menu, or go to **Format > Frame/Object** on the main menu bar to open the object dialog.

3) Click on the **Area** tab and select the type of fill you want to use for your formula from the *Fill* drop-down list (Figure 16).

4) Select the options you want to use for your formula background. The options change depending on the type of fill selected.

5) Click **OK** to save your changes and close the Object dialog.

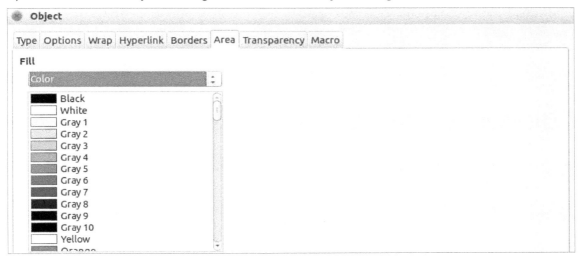

Figure 16: Object dialog – Area page

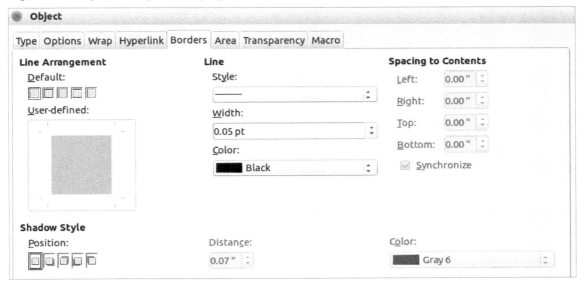

Figure 17: Object dialog – Borders page

Borders

1) In your document, select the formula where you want to change the borders.

2) Right-click on the formula and select **Object** from the context menu, or go to **Format > Frame/Object** on the main menu bar to open the object dialog.

3) Click on the **Borders** tab and select the options you want to use for your formula borders (Figure 17).

4) Click **OK** to save your changes and close the Object dialog.

Quick insertion of formulas

To quickly insert a formula into your Writer document without opening the Formula Editor and you know the markup language for the formula:

1) Enter the formula markup language into your document at the position where you want the formula.

2) Select the markup language.

3) Go to **Insert > Object** on the main menu bar and select **Formula**, or click on the **Formula** icon 🔲 on the Standard toolbar to create a formula from the selected markup language.

Note

If the **Formula** icon is not displayed on the Standard toolbar, then right-click in an empty area on the toolbar, select **Visible Buttons** from the context menu, then select **Formula** from the available options.

Math Guide

Chapter 3
Formulas in Calc, Draw & Impress

Introduction

In Calc, Draw, and Impress, formulas are inserted as OLE objects without any background (area fill) or borders. See *Chapter 1 Creating & Editing Formulas* for more information on inserting formulas into a LibreOffice module.

Each formula object is inserted into a spreadsheet, drawing, or slide as follows:

- In Calc, formulas are inserted into a selected cell in a spreadsheet with no style assigned to the formula object.
- In Draw and Impress, formulas are inserted into a central position on your drawing or slide and, by default, are assigned the drawing object style *Object with no fill and no line*. For more information on how to modify or assign drawing object styles, see the *Draw User Guide* or the *Impress User Guide*.

Anchoring formulas

Calc

A formula object can be anchored into your spreadsheet as **To Page** (default setting), or as **To Cell**. To change the anchoring type of formulas in a Calc spreadsheet:

1) Select the formula object in your spreadsheet.
2) Right-click on the formula and select **Anchor > To Page** or **To Cell** from the context menu
3) Alternatively, go to **Format > Anchor** on the main menu bar and select **To Page** or **To Cell**.

Draw and Impress

When a formula is inserted into a drawing or slide, it is inserted as a floating OLE object and is not anchored to any particular position in a drawing or slide.

Formula object properties

Formula objects in Calc, Draw, and Impress can be modified just like any other object that has been placed in your spreadsheet, drawing, or presentation, with the exception of formula object size and changing the format of any text within a formula. For more information on how to change object properties, see the *Calc User Guide*, *Draw User Guide* and *Impress User Guide*. For more information on formula object size and formatting formula text, see *Chapter 1 Creating & Editing Formulas* in this guide.

The following points will help you select which dialog to use if you want to change the properties of formula objects.

- For formula backgrounds, use the various options in the pages of the Area dialog.
- For formula borders, use the various options in the Line dialog. Note that formula borders are separate from cell borders in a Calc spreadsheet.
- To accurately re-position a formula object, use the various options in pages of the Position and Size dialog.
- In Draw and Impress, you can arrange, align, group, flip, convert, break, combine, and edit points of formula objects.
- You cannot change the text attributes of a formula object. The text used in a formula is set when you create the formula in the Formula Editor.
- Formula object size is set by the formula font size when the formula is created in the Formula Editor. The formula object size is protected in the Position and Size dialog, but this

can be deselected if you so wish. However, this is not recommended as resizing a formula object using the Position and Size dialog could lead to distortion of a formula making it difficult to read.

Formulas in charts

A chart in a Calc spreadsheet is itself an OLE object, therefore, you cannot use the Formula Editor to create and insert a formula into a chart.

To insert a formula into a chart, create the formula first using the Formula Editor and copy the formula to the clipboard. You then create your chart in Calc and paste the formula into your chart. The formula is automatically converted into the correct format for insertion into a chart.

If you want to change the formula at a later date, then you must repeat the whole process of creating, copying, and pasting.

Math Guide

Chapter 4
Customization

Introduction

This chapter explains how you can customize LibreOffice Math to suit the way you create formulas for use in LibreOffice documents. Also, refer to the *Getting Started Guide* for information on how to customize LibreOffice.

Chemical formulas

The primary purpose of Math is to create mathematical formulas, but it can also be used to write chemical formulas. However, in chemical formulas, the chemical symbols are normally written in uppercase using non-italic characters. The following table shows some examples of chemical formulas.

Construction	Example	Markup Language
Molecules	H_2SO_4	H_2 SO_4
Isotopes	$^{238}_{92}U$	U lsub 92 lsup 238
Ions	SO_4^{2-} or SO_4^{2-}	SO_4^{2-{}} *or* SO_4^{2"-"}

To create chemical formulas using Math, you have to change the font used for variables to a non-italic font. For more information on how to change fonts in a formula, see *Chapter 1 Creating and Editing Formulas*.

For reversible reactions in chemical formulas, there is no symbol you can use for a double arrow in Math. If you have a font available with correct symbols for use in chemical formulas, then you can add these symbols to the Catalog. See "Catalog customization" on page 56 for more information on how to add symbols to the Catalog.

Floating dialogs

The Formula Editor and Elements Dock can cover a large part of your document. To help create more space and/or allow you to move either the Formula Editor or Elements Dock out of the way, you turn both of them into floating dialogs.

1) Position the cursor on the frame.
2) Hold down the *Ctrl* key and double-click. This turns the Formula Editor into the Commands dialog (Figure 18) and the Elements Dock into the Elements Dock dialog (Figure 19).

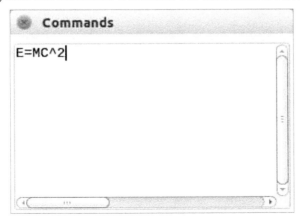

Figure 18: Commands dialog

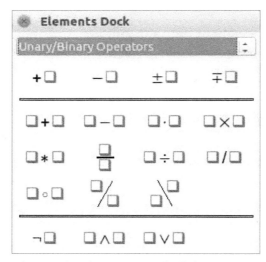

Figure 19: Elements Dock dialog

To return the Commands dialog and Elements Dock dialog back to their default positions:

1) Position the cursor on the frame of the dialog, **NOT** the title bar at the top of the of the dialog.

2) Hold down the *Ctrl* key and double-click.

Adding keyboard shortcuts

You can add keyboard shortcuts to LibreOffice to make creating documents much easier and to match your workflow. Below is an example of how to add a keyboard shortcut for inserting a Math formula into a LibreOffice document.

> **Note**
>
> When selecting new keyboards shortcuts, make sure that you do not select a keyboard shortcut that is already in use by LibreOffice or your computer system. For example, the keyboard combination *Shift+Ctrl+F2* in Calc moves the cursor to the input line where you can enter a Calc formula in the selected cell, **NOT** a Math formula.

Example keyboard shortcut

1) Go to **Tools > Customize** on the main menu bar to open the Customize dialog (Figure 20).

2) Click on the **Keyboard** tab to access the options available for adding keyboard shortcuts.

3) Select the level of the new keyboard shortcut.

   – Select *LibreOffice* so that the new keyboard shortcut can be used in all modules of LibreOffice.

   – Select *Math* to use the new keyboard shortcut in Math only.

4) In the **Category** list, select *Insert*.

5) In the **Function** list, select *Import Formula*.

6) In the **Shortcut Keys** list, select the key or keyboard combination that you want to use for your new keyboard shortcut.

7) Click **Modify** and your keyboard shortcut will appear in the **Keys** list.

8) If necessary, continue to add keyboard shortcuts using the above steps.

9) Click **OK** to save your keyboard shortcuts and close the Customize dialog.

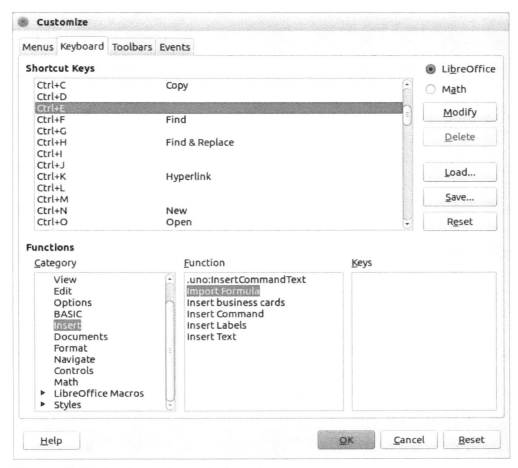

Figure 20: Customize dialog – Keyboard page

Keyboard customize options

The options for customizing keyboard shortcuts are as follows:

- **LibreOffice** – displays shortcut keys that are common to all LibreOffice modules.

- **Math**, **Writer**, **Calc**, **Draw**, or **Impress** – displays the keyboard shortcuts for the open and current LibreOffice module.

- **Shortcut Keys** – lists the shortcut keys and the associated commands. To assign or modify the shortcut key for the command selected in the *Function* list, click a shortcut in this list, and then click **Modify**.

- **Functions** – lists the function categories and the LibreOffice functions that you can assign shortcut keys to.

  - *Category* – lists the available function categories.

  - *Function* – select a function that you want to assign a shortcut key to, select a key combination in the **Shortcut Keys** list, and then click **Modify**. If the selected function already has a shortcut key, it is displayed in the *Keys* list.

  - *Keys* – displays the shortcut keys that are assigned to the selected function.

- **Modify** – assigns the key combination selected in the **Shortcut Keys** list to the command selected in the *Function* list.

- **Delete** – deletes the selected element or elements without requiring confirmation.

- **Load** – replaces the shortcut key configuration with one that was previously saved.
- **Save** – saves the current shortcut key configuration, so that you can load it later.
- **Reset** – resets modified values back to the default values.

Catalog customization

If you regularly use a symbol that is not available in Math, you can add it to the Symbols dialog (Figure 21) by opening the Edit Symbols dialog (Figure 22).

Using the Edit Symbols dialog you can add symbols to a symbol set, edit symbol sets, or modify symbol notations. You can also define new symbol sets, assign names to symbols, or modify existing symbol sets.

Adding symbols

1) Go to **Tools > Catalog** on the main menu bar or click on the **Catalog** icon ⊞ in the Tools toolbar to open the Symbols dialog.
2) Click **Edit** to open Edit Symbols dialog.
3) Select a font from the **Font:** drop-down list.
4) Select a symbol character that you want to add from the preview box. You may have to scroll down in the preview box to locate the symbol you want to use. The right preview box above the **Add** button displays the new symbol.
5) In the **Symbol:** box, type a memorable name for the symbol you are adding.
6) In the **Symbol set:** box, select a symbol set from the drop-down list to add your new symbol to, or type a new name to create a new symbol set for your new symbol.
7) If required, select a font style from the **Style:** drop-down list – Standard, *Italic*, **Bold**, or ***Bold Italic***.
8) Click **Add**, then click **OK** to close the Edit Symbols dialog. The new symbol and, if created, new symbol set are now available for use.

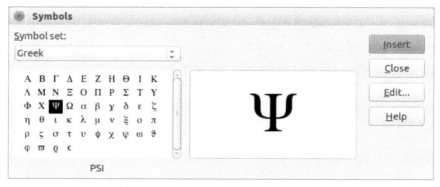

Figure 21: Symbols dialog

Note

When a new symbol is added to the catalog, you can type a percentage sign (%) followed by the new name into the markup language in the Formula Editor and your new symbol will appear in your formula. Remember that symbol names are case sensitive, for example, %prime is a different symbol to %Prime.

Note

There are numerous free fonts available that contain several symbols if you cannot find a symbol to use in the fonts already installed on your computer. For example, the STIX font was developed specially for writing mathematical and technical texts. Also, the DejaVu and Lucida fonts have a wide range of symbols that you can use.

Note

When LibreOffice is installed on a computer, only those user-defined symbols that actually occur in the document are stored with it. Sometimes it is useful to embed all the user-defined symbols, so that when the document is transferred to another computer it can be edited by another person. Go to **Tools > Options > LibreOffice Math > Settings**, uncheck the option *Embed only used symbols (smaller file size)*.This setting is only available when you are working with LibreOffice Math.

Editing symbols

Modifying symbol names

You can change the name of a symbol as follows:

1) Select the symbol name you want to change from the **Old symbol:** drop-down list. The symbol appears in the left preview pane at the bottom of the Edit Symbols dialog (Figure 22).

2) Type a new name for the symbol in the **Symbol:** text box, or select a new name from the **Symbol:** drop-down list. The new symbol name appears above the right preview pane at the bottom of the Edit Symbols dialog.

3) Click **Modify** and the symbol name is changed.

4) Click **OK** to close the Edit Symbols dialog.

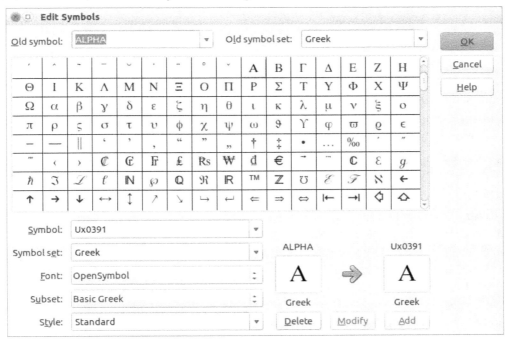

Figure 22: Edit Symbols dialog

Moving symbols

You can move a symbol from one symbol set to another as follows:

1) In the **Old symbol set:** drop-down list, select the symbol set where the symbol you want to move is located.

2) Select the symbol name you want move from the **Old symbol:** drop-down list. The symbol appears in the left preview pane at the bottom of the Edit Symbols dialog (Figure 22).

3) In the **Symbol set:** drop-down list, select the symbol set that you want to move the symbol to. The new symbol set name appears below the right preview pane at the bottom of the Edit Symbols dialog.

4) Click **Modify** and the symbol is moved to the new symbol set.

5) Click **OK** to close the Edit Symbols dialog.

Deleting symbols

You can delete a symbol from a symbol set as follows:

1) In the **Old symbol set:** drop-down list, select the symbol set from which you want to delete the symbol.

2) Select the symbol name you want delete from the **Old symbol:** drop-down list. The symbol appears in the left preview pane at the bottom of the Edit Symbols dialog (Figure 22).

3) Click **Delete** and the symbol is deleted from the symbol set without any confirmation.

4) Click **OK** to close the Edit Symbols dialog.

> **Note**
>
> The only way you can delete a symbol set is by deleting all of the symbols in that set. When you delete the last symbol from a set, the set is also deleted.

Options for editing symbols

- **Old symbol** – select the name of the current symbol. The symbol, the name of the symbol, and the set that the symbol belongs to are displayed in the left preview pane at the bottom of the Edit Symbols dialog.

- **Old symbol set** – this list box contains the name of the current symbol set. You can also select a different symbol set using this list box.

- **Symbol** – lists the names for the symbols in the current symbol set. Select a name from the list or type a name for a newly added symbol.

- **Symbol set** – this list box contains the names of all existing symbol sets. You can modify a symbol set or create a new one.

- **Font** – displays the name of the current font and enables you to select a different font.

- **Subset** – if you selected a non-symbol font in the Font list box, you can select a Unicode subset in which to place your new or edited symbol. When a subset has been selected, all symbols belonging to this subset of the current symbol set are displayed in the **Symbol** list.

- **Style** – the current style of font is displayed. You can change the font style by selecting one from the list box.

- **Add** – click this button to add the symbol shown in the right preview window to the current symbol set. It will be saved under the name displayed in the **Symbol** list. You must specify a name under **Symbol** or **Symbol set** to be able to use the **Add** button. Names cannot be used more than once.

- **Modify** – click this button to replace the name of the symbol shown in the left preview window (the old name is displayed in the **Old symbol** list) with the new name you have entered in the **Symbol** list.
- **Delete** – click this button to remove the symbol shown in the left preview window from the current symbol set. There will be confirmation of deletion. Deleting the last remaining symbol of a symbol set also deletes the symbol set.
- **Cancel** – click this button at any time to close the dialog without saving any of the changes.

Formula spacing

The grave accent (`) inserts an additional small space and the tilde (~) inserts an additional large space into formulas. However, in the basic installation of LibreOffice, these symbols are ignored when they occur at the end of a formula. If you are working with running text in a formula, it may be necessary to include spacing at the end of formulas as well. This customization is only required when you are working with a Math document and is not required when you are inserting a formula into another LibreOffice module.

To add spacing at the end of formula in Math, go to **Tools > Options > LibreOffice Math > Settings** on the main menu bar and uncheck Ignore ~ and ` at the end of the line in the *Miscellaneous Options* section.

Extensions

If you create formulas frequently in your documents, you can customize LibreOffice by adding extensions that are designed to help you create formulas. Extensions are easily installed using the Extension Manager. For more information on how to install extensions, see the *Getting Started Guide*.

One extension that is recommended for installation is **Dmaths**. This extension is designed for use in Writer and adds a mathematical macro package providing five toolbars for creating formulas. For more information on this extension, go to the website http://www.dmaths.org.

Math Guide

Chapter 5
Exporting & Importing

Math ML format

In addition to exporting documents as PDFs, as described in the *Getting Started Guide*, LibreOffice offers the possibility of exporting formulas in the MathML format. This allows you or another person to insert formulas into documents that were created in other software, for example, Microsoft Office or an internet browser.

> **Note**
>
> Some internet browsers do not fully support the MathML format and your formula may not display correctly.

If you are working on a Math document, go to **File > Save as** on the main menu bar or use the keyboard combination *Ctrl+Shift+S* to open the Save as dialog. Select MathML from the list of available file formats in **File type:** to save your formula as MathML.

If you are working in another LibreOffice module, right-click on the formula object and select **Save copy as** from the context menu to open the Save as dialog. Select MathML from the list of available file formats in **File type:** to save your formula object as MathML.

Microsoft file formats

To control how formulas in Microsoft format are imported and exported using LibreOffice, go to **Tools > Options > Load/Save > Microsoft Office** on the main menu bar and select or deselect the options for **MathType to LibreOffice Math or reverse**.

- *[L]: Load and convert the object*
- *[S]: Convert and save the object*

[L]: Load and convert the object

Select this option if Microsoft OLE objects are to be converted into the specified LibreOffice OLE object when a Microsoft document is opened in LibreOffice. For formulas, any embedded MathType objects must not exceed the MathType 3.1 specifications to be successfully loaded and converted. Information on MathType format can be found on the website http://www.dessci.com/en.

Any formulas created using the Microsoft Office Math Markup Language (OMML) cannot be converted when the document is loaded into LibreOffice regardless of whether the *[L]: Load and convert the object* option is selected. OMML is normally used in the later versions of Microsoft Office that use the .docx format for documents.

If a document containing OMML formulas has been saved in .docx format and then converted to the older .doc format, then any OMML objects are converted into graphics, which will be displayed in LibreOffice as graphics.

[S]: Convert and save the object

Select this option if LibreOffice OLE objects are to be converted and saved in Microsoft file format. LibreOffice converts any formulas into a format that can be read and modified by Microsoft Equation Editor and MathType.

When this option is not selected, the formula is treated as an OLE object on conversion into a .doc format and remains linked to LibreOffice. A double-click on the object in Microsoft Office will attempt to launch LibreOffice.

If a LibreOffice document is saved in the .docx format, formulas are not converted, whether this option is selected or not.

Math Guide

Appendix A
Commands Reference

Introduction

This appendix lists all the operators and commands that are available for use in the Formula Editor when you are creating your formulas.

The more common operators and commands can be entered by clicking on the appropriate icon in the Elements Dock. Where there is no icon displayed in the following tables for the Elements Dock, then you have to enter the operator or command into the Formula Editor using markup language.

> **Note**
>
> In the markup language shown in the following tables, you have to replace the place holder <?> with the value you want to use in your formulas.

Unary/binary operator commands

To access the icons used for entering markup language for unary/binary operator commands into the Formula Editor, select **Unary/Binary Operators** from the drop-down list at the top of the Elements Dock.

Operation	Markup language	Example formula	Elements Dock
Plus	+	$+1$	
Minus	-	-1	
Plus/minus	+- *or* plusminus	± 1	
Minus/plus	-+ *or* minusplus	∓ 1	
Addition	<?> + <?>	$A+B$	
Subtraction	<?> - <?>	$A-B$	
Multiplication (Dot)	<?> cdot <?>	$A \cdot B$	
Multiplication	<?> times <?>	$A \times B$	
Multiplication (*)	<?> * <?>	$A * B$	
Division (Fraction)	{<?>} over {<?>}	$\frac{A}{B}$	
Division	<?> div <?>	$A \div B$	
Division (Slash)	<?> / <?> *or* <?> slash <?>	A/B	

Operation	Markup language	Example formula	Elements Dock
Division (Wideslash)	`{<?>} wideslash {<?>}`	A/B	
Division (Counter Wideslash)	`<?> widebslash <?>`	$\backslash \begin{smallmatrix}B\\A\end{smallmatrix}$	
Concatenate	`<?> circ <?>`	$A \circ B$	
Boolean NOT	`neg <?>`	$\neg A$	
Boolean AND	`<?> and <?>` or `<?> & <?>`	$A \wedge B$	
Boolean OR	`<?> or <?>`	$A \vee B$	
Backslash	`<?> bslash <?>`	$A \backslash B$	
Slash in circle	`<?> odivide <?>`	$A \oslash B$	
Small multiply symbol in circle	`<?> odot <?>`	$A \odot B$	
Subtract symbol in circle	`<?> ominus <?>`	$A \ominus B$	
Add symbol in circle	`<?> oplus <?>`	$A \oplus B$	
Multiply symbol in circle	`<?> otimes <?>`	$A \otimes B$	
User defined binary operator	`<?> boper ????? <?>`	$monOp\,B$	
User defined unary operator	`<?> uoper ????? <?>`	$A\,monOp\,B$	

Relation commands

To access the icons used for entering markup language for relations commands into the Formula Editor, select **Relations** from the drop-down list at the top of the Elements Dock.

Operation	Markup language	Example formula	Elements Dock
Is equal	`<?> = <?>`	$A = B$	
Is not equal	`<?> <> <?>` or `<?> neq <?>`	$A \neq B$	
Is less than	`<?> < <?>` or `<?> lt <?>`	$A < B$	

Operation	Markup language	Example formula	Elements Dock
Is less than or equal to	`<?> <= <?>`	$A \leq B$	⬜ ≤ ⬜
Is less than or equal to	`<?> leslant <?>`	$A \leqslant B$	⬜ ⩽ ⬜
Is greater than	`<?> > <?>` or `<?> gt <?>`	$A > B$	⬜ > ⬜
Is greater than or equal to	`<?> >= <?>`	$A \geq B$	⬜ ≥ ⬜
Is greater than or equal to	`<?> geslant <?>`	$A \geqslant B$	⬜ ⩾ ⬜
Is much less than	`<?> << <?>` or `<?> ll <?>`	$A \ll B$	⬜ ≪ ⬜
Is much greater than	`<?> >> <?>` or `<?> gg <?>`	$A \gg B$	⬜ ≫ ⬜
Is approximately equal	`<?> approx <?>`	$A \approx B$	⬜ ≈ ⬜
Is similar to	`<?> sim <?>`	$A \sim B$	⬜ ~ ⬜
Is similar to or equal	`<?> simeq <?>`	$A \simeq B$	⬜ ≃ ⬜
Is congruent to	`<?> equiv <?>`	$A \equiv B$	⬜ ≡ ⬜
Is proportional to	`<?> prop <?>`	$A \propto B$	⬜ ∝ ⬜
Is parallel to	`<?> parallel <?>`	$A \| B$	⬜ ∥ ⬜
Is orthogonal to	`<?> ortho <?>`	$A \perp B$	⬜ ⊥ ⬜
Divides	`<?> divides <?>`	$A	B$	⬜	⬜
Does not divide	`<?> ndivides <?>`	$A \nmid B$	⬜ ∤ ⬜
Toward	`<?> toward <?>`	$A \rightarrow B$	⬜ → ⬜
Double arrow left	`<?> dlarrow <?>`	$A \Leftarrow B$	⬜ ⇐ ⬜
Double arrow left and right	`<?> dlrarrow <?>`	$A \Leftrightarrow B$	⬜ ⇔ ⬜
Double arrow right	`<?> drarrow <?>`	$A \Rightarrow B$	⬜ ⇒ ⬜
Precedes	`<?> prec <?>`	$A \prec B$	⬜ ≺ ⬜

Operation	Markup language	Example formula	Elements Dock
Succeeds	`<?> succ <?>`	$A \succ B$	
Precedes or equal to	`<?> preccurlyeq <?>`	$A \preccurlyeq B$	
Succeeds or equal to	`<?> succcurlyeq <?>`	$A \succcurlyeq B$	
Precedes or equivalent to	`<?> precsim <?>`	$A \precsim B$	
Succeeds or equivalent to	`<?> succsim <?>`	$A \succsim B$	
Not precedes	`<?> nprec <?>`	$A \nprec B$	
Not succeeds	`<?> nsucc <?>`	$A \nsucc B$	
Definition	`<?> def <?>`	$A \overset{\text{def}}{=} B$	
Corresponding symbol image of	`<?> transl <?>`	$A \multimapdotbothA B$	
Corresponding symbol original of	`<?> transr <?>`	$A \multimapdotbothB B$	

Set operation commands

To access the icons used for entering markup language for set operation commands into the Formula Editor, select **Set Operations** from the drop-down list at the top of the Elements Dock.

Operation	Markup language	Example formula	Elements Dock
Is in	`<?> in <?>`	$A \in B$	
Is not in	`<?> notin <?>`	$A \notin B$	
Owns	`<?> owns <?>` or `<?> ni <?>`	$A \ni B$	
Intersection	`<?> intersection <?>`	$A \cap B$	
Union	`<?> union <?>`	$A \cup B$	
Difference	`<?> setminus <?>` or `<?> bslash <?>`	$A \setminus B$	

Operation	Markup language	Example formula	Elements Dock
Quotient set (slash) between characters	`<?> slash <?>`	A/B	☐/☐
Subset	`<?> subset <?>`	$A \subset B$	☐⊂☐
Subset or equal to	`<?> subseteq <?>`	$A \subseteq B$	☐⊆☐
Superset	`<?> supset <?>`	$A \supset B$	☐⊃☐
Superset or equal to	`<?> supseteq <?>`	$A \supseteq B$	☐⊇☐
Not subset	`<?> nsubset <?>`	$A \not\subset B$	☐⊄☐
Not subset or equal to	`<?> nsubseteq <?>`	$A \nsubseteq B$	☐⊈☐
Not superset	`<?> nsupset <?>`	$A \not\supset B$	☐⊅☐
Not superset or equal to	`<?> nsupseteq <?>`	$A \nsupseteq B$	☐⊉☐
Empty set	`emptyset`	$\emptyset$	∅
Aleph (cardinal numbers)	`aleph`	$\aleph$	ℵ
Natural numbers set	`setN`	$\mathbb{N}$	ℕ
Integers set	`setZ`	$\mathbb{Z}$	ℤ
Set of rational numbers	`setQ`	$\mathbb{Q}$	ℚ
Real numbers set	`setR`	$\mathbb{R}$	ℝ
Complex numbers set	`setC`	$\mathbb{C}$	ℂ

Functions

To access the icons used for entering markup language for function commands into the Formula Editor, select **Functions** from the drop-down list at the top of the Elements Dock.

Operation	Markup language	Example formula	Elements Dock
Absolute value	`abs{<?>}`	$\lvert A \rvert$	|☐|
Factorial	`fact{<?>}`	$A!$	☐!

Operation	Markup language	Example formula	Elements Dock
Square root	`sqrt{<?>}`	$\sqrt{A}$	
Nth root	`nroot{<?>}{<?>}`	$\sqrt[A]{B}$	
Power	`<?>^{<?>}`	A^B	
Natural exponential function	`func e^{<?>}`	e^A	
Natural logarithm	`ln(<?>)`	$\ln(A)$	$\ln(\square)$
Exponential function	`exp(<?>)`	$\exp(A)$	$\exp(\square)$
Logarithm	`log(<?>)`	$\log(A)$	$\log(\square)$
Sine	`sin(<?>)`	$\sin(A)$	$\sin(\square)$
Cosine	`cos(<?>)`	$\cos(A)$	$\cos(\square)$
Tangent	`tan(<?>)`	$\tan(A)$	$\tan(\square)$
Cotangent	`cot(<?>)`	$\cot(A)$	$\cot(\square)$
Hyperbolic sine	`sinh(<?>)`	$\sinh(A)$	$\sinh(\square)$
Hyperbolic cosine	`cosh(<?>)`	$\cosh(A)$	$\cosh(\square)$
Hyperbolic tangent	`tanh(<?>)`	$\tanh(A)$	$\tanh(\square)$
Hyperbolic cotangent	`coth(<?>)`	$\coth(A)$	$\coth(\square)$
Inverse sine or arcsine	`arcsin(<?>)`	$\arcsin(A)$	$\arcsin(\square)$
Inverse cosine or arccosine	`arccos(<?>)`	$\arccos(A)$	$\arccos(\square)$
Inverse tangent or arctangent	`arctan(<?>)`	$\arctan(A)$	$\arctan(\square)$
Inverse cotangent or arccotangent	`arccot(<?>)`	$\text{arccot}(A)$	$\text{arccot}(\square)$
Inverse or area hyperbolic sine	`arsinh(<?>)`	$\text{arsinh}(A)$	$\text{arsinh}(\square)$

Operation	Markup language	Example formula	Elements Dock
Inverse or area hyperbolic cosine	`arcosh(<?>)`	$\mathrm{arcosh}(A)$	**arcosh** (□)
Inverse or area hyperbolic tangent	`artanh(<?>)`	$\mathrm{artanh}(A)$	**artanh** (□)
Inverse or area hyperbolic cotangent	`arcoth(<?>)`	$\mathrm{arcoth}(A)$	**arcoth** (□)
Back epsilon	`backepsilon`	$\backepsilon$	
Subscript	`<?> sub <?>`	A_B	

Operators

To access the icons used for entering markup language for operator commands into the Formula Editor, select **Operators** from the drop-down list at the top of the Elements Dock.

Operation	Markup language	Example formula	Elements Dock
Limes	`lim <?>`	$\lim A$	**lim** □
Limes subscript bottom	`lim from{<?>} <?>`	$\lim_{A} B$	**lim** □ □
Limes superscript top	`lim to{<?>} <?>`	$\lim^{A} B$	□ **lim** □
Limes sup/sub script	`lim from{<?>} to{<?>} <?>`	$\lim_{A}^{B} C$	□ **lim** □ □
Limes inferior	`liminf <?>`	$\lim\inf A$	
Limes superior	`limsup <?>`	$\lim\sup A$	
Sum	`sum <?>`	$\sum a$	$\sum$ □
Sum subscript bottom	`sum from{<?>} <?>`	$\sum_{A} B$	$\sum$ □ □

Operation	Markup language	Example formula	Elements Dock
Sum superscript top	`sum to{<?>} <?>`	$\sum^{A} B$	
Sum sup/sub script	`sum from{<?>} to{<?>} <?>`	$\sum_{A}^{B} C$	
Product	`prod <?>`	$\prod A$	
Product subscript bottom	`prod from{<?>} <?>`	$\prod_{A} B$	
Product superscript top	`prod to{<?>} <?>`	$\prod^{A} B$	
Product sup/sub script	`prod from{<?>} to{<?>} <?>`	$\prod_{A}^{B} C$	
Coproduct	`coprod <?>`	$\coprod A$	
Coproduct subscript bottom	`coprod from{<?>} <?>`	$\coprod_{A} B$	
Coproduct superscript top	`coprod to{<?>} <?>`	$\coprod^{A} B$	
Coproduct sup/sub script	`coprod from{<?>} to{<?>} <?>`	$\coprod_{A}^{B} C$	
Integral	`int <?>`	$\int A$	

Operation	Markup language	Example formula	Elements Dock
Integral subscript bottom	`int from{<?>} <?>`	$\int_A B$	
Integral superscript top	`int to{<?>} <?>`	$\int^A B$	
Integral sup/sub script	`int from{<?>} to{<?>} <?>`	$\int_A^B C$	
Double integral	`iint <?>`	$\iint A$	
Double integral subscript bottom	`iint from{<?>} <?>`	$\iint_A B$	
Double integral superscript top	`iint to{<?>} <?>`	$\iint^A B$	
Double integral sup/sub script	`iint from{<?>} to{<?>} <?>`	$\iint_A^B C$	
Triple integral	`iiint <?>`	$\iiint A$	
Triple integral subscript bottom	`iiint from{<?>} <?>`	$\iiint_A B$	
Triple integral superscript top	`iiint to{<?>} <?>`	$\iiint^A B$	

Operation	Markup language	Example formula	Elements Dock
Triple integral sup/sub script	iiint from{<?>} to{<?>} <?>	$\iiint_{A}^{B} C$	
Curve integral	lint <?>	$\oint A$	
Curve integral subscript bottom	lint from{<?>} <?>	$\oint_{A} B$	
Curve integral superscript top	lint to{<?>} <?>	$\oint^{A} B$	
Curve integral sup/sub script	lint from{<?>} to{<?>} <?>	$\oint_{A}^{B} C$	
Double curve integral	llint <?>	$\oiint A$	
Double curve integral subscript bottom	llint from{<?>} <?>	$\oiint_{A} B$	
Double curve integral superscript top	llint to{<?>} <?>	$\oiint^{A} B$	
Double curve integral sup/sub script	llint from{<?>} to{<?>} <?>	$\oiint_{A}^{B} C$	
Triple curve integral	lllint <?>	$\oiiint A$	
Triple curve integral subscript bottom	lllint from{<?>} <?>	$\oiiint_{A} B$	

Operation	Markup language	Example formula	Elements Dock
Triple curve integral superscript top	`lllint to{<?>} <?>`	$\oiiint^{A} B$	
Triple curve integral sup/sub script	`lllint from{<?>} to{<?>} <?>`	$\oiiint_{A}^{B} C$	

Note

For customized operators, use the command `oper` followed by your custom operator.

For example, entering `oper OP from 0 to 1` A will give the formula $OP_{0}^{1} A$.

Attributes

To access the icons used for entering markup language for attribute commands into the Formula Editor, select **Attributes** from the drop-down list at the top of the Elements Dock, or click the **Attributes** icon in the Elements dialog.

Operation	Markup language	Example formula	Elements Dock
Acute accent	`acute <?>`	$\acute{A}$	
Grave accent	`grave <?>`	$\grave{A}$	
Breve	`breve <?>`	$\breve{A}$	
Circle	`circle <?>`	$\mathring{A}$	
Dot	`dot <?>`	$\dot{A}$	
Double dot	`ddot <?>`	$\ddot{A}$	
Triple dot	`dddot <?>`	$\dddot{A}$	
Line above	`bar <?>`	$\bar{A}$	
Vector arrow	`vec <?>`	$\vec{A}$	

Operation	Markup language	Example formula	Elements Dock
Tilde	tilde <?>	$\tilde{A}$	
Circumflex	hat <?>	$\hat{A}$	
Reverse circumflex	check <?>	$\check{A}$	
Large vector arrow	widevec {<?>}	$\overrightarrow{AB}$	
Large tilde	widetilde {<?>}	$\widetilde{AB}$	
Large circumflex	widehat {<?>}	$\widehat{AB}$	
Line over	overline {<?>}	$\overline{AB}$	
Line below	underline {<?>}	$\underline{AB}$	
Line through	overstrike {<?>}	$\overline{AB}$	
Transparent (blank placeholder to create space)	phantom {<?>}		hide
Bold font	bold <?>	**AB**	**B**
Not bold font	nbold <?>	AB	
Italic font	ital <?> or italic <?>	*AB*	*I*
Not italic font	nitalic <?>	AB	
Resize	size <?> {<?>}	*AB*	size
Change font	font <?> {<?>}	*AB*	font
Color black	color black {<?>}	*AB*	**black**
Color blue	color blue {<?>}	*AB*	blue
Color green	color green {<?>}	*AB*	green
Color red	color red {<?>}	*AB*	red

Operation	Markup language	Example formula	Elements Dock
Color cyan	color cyan {<?>}		cyan
Color magenta	color magenta {<?>}	AB	magenta
Color yellow	color yellow {<?>}		
Color gray	color gray {<?>}	AB	gray
Color lime	color lime {<?>}		lime
Color maroon	color maroon {<?>}	AB	maroon
Color navy	color navy {<?>}	AB	navy
Color olive	color olive {<?>}	AB	olive
Color purple	color purple {<?>}	AB	purple
Color silver	color silver {<?>}	AB	silver
Color teal	color teal {<?>}	AB	teal

Note

The font command changes the font type The first placeholder is replaced with the name of the font and the second placeholder is replaced with your formula values or text. The default fonts you can use are Serif, Sans, or Fixed. If you have added custom fonts to Math (see *Chapter 1 Creating & Editing Formulas*), then you can replace the first placeholder with the custom font name.

Brackets

To access the icons used for entering markup language for bracket commands into the Formula Editor, select **Brackets** from the drop-down list at the top of the Elements Dock.

Operation	Markup language	Example formula	Elements Dock
Group brackets (not displayed in formula)	{<?>}	AB	□
Round brackets	(<?>)	(AB)	(□)
Left round bracket only	\(<?>	$(A$	

Operation	Markup language	Example formula	Elements Dock
Right round bracket only	`<?>\)`	$A\,)$	
Square brackets	`[<?>]`	$[AB]$	[▢]
Left square bracket only	`\[<?>`	$[A$	
Right square bracket only	`<?>\]`	$A]$	
Double square brackets	`ldbracket <?> rdbracket`	$[\![AB]\!]$	[▢]
Left double square bracket only	`\ldbracket <?>`	$[\![A$	
Right double square bracket only	`<?> \rdbracket`	$A]\!]$	
Braces	`lbrace <?> rbrace`	$\{AB\}$	{ ▢ }
Left brace only	`\lbrace <?>`	$\{A$	
Right brace only	`<?> \rbrace`	$A\}$	
Angle brackets	`langle <?> rangle`	$\langle AB\rangle$	⟨ ▢ ⟩
Left angle bracket only	`\langle <?>`	$\langle A$	
Right angle bracket only	`<?> \rangle`	$A\rangle$	
Operator brackets	`langle <?> mline <?> rangle`	$\langle AB\vert CD\rangle$	⟨ ▢ | ▢ ⟩
Ceiling (upper half square brackets)	`lceil <?> rceil`	$\lceil AB\rceil$	⌈ ▢ ⌉
Left ceiling only	`\lceil <?>`	$\lceil A$	
Right ceiling only	`<?> \rceil`	$A\rceil$	
Floor (lower half square brackets)	`lfloor <?> rfloor`	$\lfloor AB\rfloor$	⌊ ▢ ⌋
Left floor only	`\lfloor <?>`	$\lfloor A$	
Right floor only	`<?> \rfloor`	$A\rfloor$	

Operation	Markup language	Example formula	Elements Dock
Single lines	lline <?> rline	$\lvert AB \rvert$	
Left single line only	\lline <?>	$\lvert A$	
Right single line only	<?> \rline	$A \rvert$	
Double lines	ldline <?> rdline	$\lVert AB \rVert$	
Left double line only	\ldline <?>	$\lVert A$	
Right double line only	<?> \rdline	$A \rVert$	
Scalable round brackets	left (<?> right)	$\left(\dfrac{A}{B} \right)$	
Scalable left round bracket only	left (<?> right none	$\left(\dfrac{A}{B} \right.$	
Scalable right round bracket only	left none <?> right)	$\left. \dfrac{A}{B} \right)$	
Scalable square brackets	left [<?> right]	$\left[\dfrac{A}{B} \right]$	
Scalable left square bracket only	left [<?> right none	$\left[\dfrac{A}{B} \right.$	
Scalable right square bracket only	left none <?> right]	$\left. \dfrac{A}{B} \right]$	
Scalable double square brackets	left ldbracket <?> right rdbracket	$\left\llbracket \dfrac{A}{B} \right\rrbracket$	
Scalable left double square bracket only	left ldbracket <?> right none	$\left\llbracket \dfrac{A}{B} \right.$	
Scalable right double square bracket only	left none <?> right rdbracket	$\left. \dfrac{A}{B} \right\rrbracket$	
Scalable braces	left lbrace <?> right rbrace	$\left\{ \dfrac{A}{B} \right\}$	

Operation	Markup language	Example formula	Elements Dock
Scalable left brace only	`left lbrace {<?>} right none`	$\left\{\dfrac{A}{B}\right.$	
Scalable right brace only	`left none {<?>} right rbrace`	$\left.\dfrac{A}{B}\right\}$	
Scalable angle brackets	`left langle <?> right rangle`	$\left\langle\dfrac{A}{B}\right\rangle$	
Scalable left angle bracket only	`left langle {<?>} right none`	$\left\langle\dfrac{A}{B}\right.$	
Scalable right angle bracket only	`left none {<?>} right rangle`	$\left.\dfrac{A}{B}\right\rangle$	
Scalable operator brackets	`left langle <?> mline <?> right none`	$\left\langle\dfrac{A}{B}\middle|\dfrac{C}{D}\right\rangle$	
Scalable left operator bracket	`left langle <?> mline <?> right none`	$\left\langle\dfrac{A}{B}\middle|\dfrac{C}{D}\right.$	
Scalable right operator bracket	`left none <?> mline <?> right rangle`	$\left.\dfrac{A}{B}\middle|\dfrac{C}{D}\right\rangle$	
Scalable ceiling (upper half square brackets)	`left lceil <?> right rceil`	$\left\lceil\dfrac{A}{B}\right\rceil$	
Scalable left ceiling	`left lceil <?> right none`	$\left\lceil\dfrac{A}{B}\right.$	
Scalable right ceiling	`left none <?> right rceil`	$\left.\dfrac{A}{B}\right\rceil$	
Scalable floor (lower half square brackets)	`left lfloor <?> right rfloor`	$\left\lfloor\dfrac{A}{B}\right\rfloor$	
Scalable left floor	`left lfloor <?> right none`	$\left\lfloor\dfrac{A}{B}\right.$	
Scalable right floor	`left none <?> right rfloor`	$\left.\dfrac{A}{B}\right\rfloor$	

Operation	Markup language	Example formula	Elements Dock
Scalable single lines	`left lline <?> right rline`	$\left\| \dfrac{A}{B} \right\|$	
Scalable left single line	`left lline <?> right none`	$\left\| \dfrac{A}{B} \right.$	
Scalable right single line	`left none <?> right rline`	$\left. \dfrac{A}{B} \right\|$	
Scalable double lines	`left ldline <?> right rdline`	$\left\| \dfrac{A}{B} \right\|$	
Scalable left double line	`left ldline <?> right none`	$\left\| \dfrac{A}{B} \right.$	
Scalable right double line	`left none <?> right rdline`	$\left. \dfrac{A}{B} \right\|$	
Scalable top brace	`{<?>} overbrace {<?>}`	$\overbrace{ABC}^{D}$	
Scalable bottom brace	`{<?>} underbrace {<?>}`	$\underbrace{ABC}_{D}$	

Formats

To access the icons used for entering markup language for format commands into the Formula Editor, select **Formats** from the drop-down list at the top of the Elements Dock.

Operation	Markup language	Example formula	Elements Dock
Power (superscript right)	`<?>^{<?>}` or `<?>sup{<?>}` or `<?>rsup{<?>}`	20^{10}	
Subscript right	`<?>_{<?>}` or `<?>sub{<?>}` or `<?>rsub{<?>}`	20_{10}	
Superscript left	`<?>lsup{<?>}`	$^{10}20$	
Subscript left	`<?>lsub{<?>}`	$_{10}20$	

Operation	Markup language	Example formula	Elements Dock
Superscript center	`<?>csup{<?>}`	$\overset{10}{20}$	
Subscript center	`<?>csub{<?>}`	$\underset{10}{20}$	
New line	`newline`	123 *CD*	
Small gap	`` ` ``	123 456	
Blank or large gap	`~`	123 456	
No space (suppresses space between elements)	`nospace {<?>}`	12+4+5	
Align left	`alignl <?>`	*ABC* *D*	**left**
Align center	`alignc <?>`	*ABC* *D*	**center**
Align right	`alignr <?>`	*ABC* *D*	**right**
Vertical stack (2 elements)	`binom{<?>}{<?>}`	*AB* 12	
Vertical stack (more than 2 elements)	`stack{<?> # <?> # <?>}`	*AB* 12 *CD*	
Matrix stack	`matrix{<?> # <?> ## <?> # <?>}`	*AB* 12 34 *CD*	

Note

By default, text characters are aligned to the center in a formula. Use the `alignl` and `alignr` commands to align text characters in a formula to the left or right when a formula has more than one line. You can also use the align commands in conjunction with the stack commands to align multi-line formulas on a specific formula element, for example, the equals sign (=).

Others

To access the icons used for entering markup language for other commands into the Formula Editor, select **Others** from the drop-down list at the top of the Elements Dock, or click the **Others** icon in the Elements dialog.

Operation	Markup language	Example formula	Elements Dock
Placeholder	`<?>`		
Infinity	`infinity` or `infty`	∞	∞
Partial derivative or set margin	`partial`	∂	∂
Nabla vector operator	`nabla`	∇	∇
Existential quantifier, there is at least one	`exists`	∃	∃
Existential quantifier, there does not exist	`notexists`	∄	∄
Universal quantifier, for all	`forall`	∀	∀
H-bar constant	`hbar`	ℏ	ℏ
Lambda bar	`lambdabar`	ƛ	ƛ
Real part of a complex number	`re`	ℜ	ℜ
Imaginary part of a complex number	`im`	ℑ	ℑ
Weierstrass p function	`wp`	℘	℘
Left arrow	`leftarrow`	←	←
Right arrow	`rightarrow`	→	→
Up arrow	`uparrow`	↑	↑
Down arrow	`downarrow`	↓	↓
Ellipsis	`dotslow`	⋯	⋯

Operation	Markup language	Example formula	Elements Dock
Math axis ellipsis	`dotsaxis`	⋯	▪ ▪ ▪
Vertical ellipsis	`dotsvert`	⋮	▪ ▪ ▪
Upward diagonal ellipsis	`dotsup` or `dotsdiag`	⋰	▪ ▪ ▪
Downward diagonal ellipsis	`dotsdown`	⋱	▪ ▪ ▪
Back epsilon	`backepsilon`	϶	

Greek characters

Greek characters are normally entered into a formula using the Symbols dialog (see *Chapter 1 Creating & Editing Formulas* for more information). However, if you know the name of the Greek character, you can type a percentage sign (%) followed by the name of the Greek character into the Formula Editor.

For uppercase Greek characters, type the name using uppercase characters, for example `%BETA` Β (see Table 3 for a full list of uppercase Greek characters). For lowercase Greek characters, type the name using lowercase characters, for example `%beta` β (see Table 4 for a full list of lowercase Greek characters)

Italic Greek characters can also be entered into a formula by typing the character i after the percentage sign (%) and before the name of the Greek character, for example, `%iPI` Π for uppercase and `%ipi` for lowercase π . See Table 5 for a full list of italic uppercase Greek characters and Table 6 for a full list of italic lowercase Greek characters.

> **Note**
>
> In localized versions of LibreOffice, the names of Greek characters are also localized. If a document is not localized to the same language, then the names of Greek characters in the following tables may not work correctly. If this happens, you can use the Symbols dialog to select the required Greek character. When selected in the Symbols dialog, the name of the Greek character is displayed at the bottom of the Symbols dialog in the correct language. See *Chapter 1 Creating & Editing Formulas* for more information on Greek characters and the Symbols dialog.

Table 3: Uppercase Greek characters

%ALPHA	A	%BETA	B	%GAMMA	Γ	%DELTA	Δ
%EPSILON	E	%ZETA	Z	%ETA	H	%THETA	Θ
%IOTA	I	%KAPPA	K	%LAMBDA	Λ	%MU	M
%NU	N	%XI	Ξ	%OMICRON	O	%PI	Π
%RHO	P	%SIGMA	Σ	%TAU	T	%UPSILON	Y
%PHI	Φ	%CHI	X	%PSI	Ψ	%OMEGA	Ω

Table 4: Lowercase Greek characters

%alpha	α	%beta	β	%gamma	γ	%delta	δ
%varepsilon	ε	%zeta	ζ	%eta	η	%theta	θ
%iota	ι	%kappa	κ	%lambda	λ	%mu	μ
%nu	ν	%xi	ξ	%omicron	ο	%pi	π
%rho	ρ	%varsigma	ς	%sigma	σ	%tau	τ
%upsilon	υ	%varphi	φ	%chi	χ	%psi	ψ
%omega	ω	%vartheta	ϑ	%phi	φ	%varpi	ϖ
%varrho	ϱ	%epsilon	ε				

Table 5: Uppercase italic Greek characters

%iALPHA	*A*	%iBETA	*B*	%iGAMMA	*Γ*	%iDELTA	*Δ*
%iEPSILON	*E*	%iZETA	*Z*	%iETA	*H*	%iTHETA	
%iIOTA		%iKAPPA	*K*	%iLAMBDA	*Λ*	%iMU	*M*
%iNU	*N*	%iXI	*Ξ*	%iOMICRON	*O*	%iPI	*Π*
%iRHO	*P*	%iSIGMA	*Σ*	%iTAU	*T*	%iUPSILON	*Y*
%iPHI	*Φ*	%iCHI	*X*	%iPSI	*Ψ*	%iOMEGA	*Ω*

Table 6: Lowercase italic Greek characters

%ialpha	*α*	%ibeta	*β*	%igamma	*γ*	%idelta	*δ*
%ivarepsilon	*ε*	%izeta	*ζ*	%ieta	*η*	%itheta	*θ*
%iiota	*ι*	%ikappa	*κ*	%ilambda	*λ*	%imu	*μ*
%inu	*ν*	%ixi	*ξ*	%iomicron	*ο*	%ipi	*π*
%irho	*ρ*	%ivarsigma	*ς*	%isigma	*σ*	%itau	*τ*
%iupsilon	*υ*	%ivarphi	*φ*	%ichi	*χ*	%ipsi	*ψ*
%iomega	*ω*	%ivartheta	*ϑ*	%iphi	*φ*	%ivarpi	*ϖ*
%ivarrho	*ϱ*	%iepsilon	*ε*				

Special characters

Special characters are normally entered into a formula using the Symbols dialog (see *Chapter 1 Creating & Editing Formulas* for more information). However, if you know the name of the special character, you can type a percentage sign (%) followed by the name of the special character into the Formula Editor. Table 7 Shows the full list of special characters that are available in LibreOffice.

Note

In localized versions of LibreOffice, the names of special characters are also localized. If a document is not localized to the same language, then the names of special characters in the following table may not work correctly. If this happens, you can use the Symbols dialog to select the required special character. When selected in the Symbols dialog, the name of the special character is displayed at the bottom of the Symbols dialog in the correct language. See *Chapter 1 Creating & Editing Formulas* for more information on special characters and the Symbols dialog.

Table 7: Special characters

%perthousand	‰	%tendto	→	%element	∈
%noelement	∉	%infinite	∞	%angle	∡
%and	∧	%or	∨	%notequal	≠
%identical	≡	%strictlylessthan	≪	%strictlygreaterthan	≫

Reserved words

A reserved word is a word that is used by LibreOffice as a command in the Math markup language and it cannot be used as a variable name or entered into a formula as text. However, if you want to use a reserved word as text in a formula then you must place the reserved word between double quotes.

For example, you want to use the word "purple" in a formula, but do not want the formula elements to be changed to the color purple. If you simply type A purple B in the Formula Editor, the resulting formula is $A \, ¿ \, B$, which is incorrect and the error is shown by the upside question mark. To correct this error, type A "purple" B in the Formula Editor using double quotes each side of the word purple and the resulting correct formula is $A \, purple \, B$.

The reserved words used in Math are listed in the above tables for commands in markup language.